Kyokai : A Japanese Technique for Articulating Space

Editorial supervision by Kengo Kuma
監修 隈 研吾
Photographs by Kiyoshi Takai
写真 高井 潔

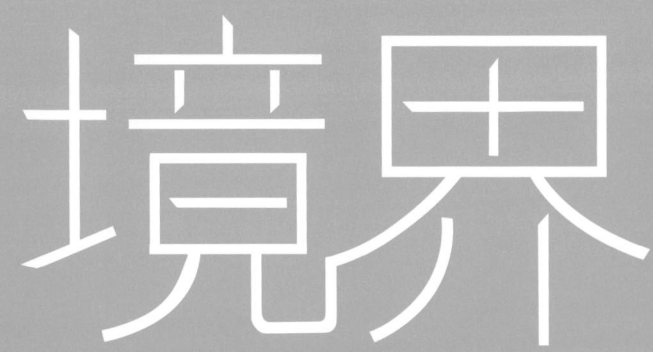

境界
世界を変える日本の空間操作術

Tankosha
淡交社

Kyokai : A Japanese Technique for Articulating Space

Editorial supervision by Kengo Kuma
監修 隈 研吾
Photographs by Kiyoshi Takai
写真 高井 潔

境界
世界を変える日本の空間操作術

Tankosha
淡交社

Kyokai: A Japanese Technique for Articulating Space

Published in 2010 by Tankosha Publishing Co.,Ltd.
Copyright 2010, Tankosha Publishing Co., Ltd, All Rights Reserved.

Printed in Japan
ISBN978-4-473-03645-2

境界
世界を変える日本の空間操作術

Kyokai
A Japanese Technique for Articulating Space

Editorial supervision by Kengo Kuma
監修 隈 研吾

Photographs by Kiyoshi Takai
写真 高井 潔

Tankosha
淡交社

目次
Contents

日本的な「関係性の建築」の時代へ
Toward a Japanese-Style Architecture of Relationships
　　　　　　　　　　隈 研吾　Kengo Kuma　　　　　6

第 1 章　内と外の曖昧な境界
Chapter. 1　　　Vague Boundaries Between Interior and Exterior　　19

   窓　　　　　Window　　　　　　　　　　20
   蔀戸　　　　Hinged Shutter　　　　　　　24
   格子　　　　Lattice　　　　　　　　　　　26
   犬矢来　　　Protective Screen　　　　　　28
   垣根　　　　Fence or Hedge　　　　　　　30
   塀　　　　　Wall　　　　　　　　　　　　34
   門　　　　　Gate　　　　　　　　　　　　36
   玄関　　　　Entrance　　　　　　　　　　40
   土間・三和土　Earth or Mortar Floored Areas　42
   通り庭　　　Open Corridor　　　　　　　　46
   縁側　　　　Veranda　　　　　　　　　　　48
   軒　　　　　Eaves　　　　　　　　　　　　53
   壁　　　　　Wall　　　　　　　　　　　　55
   屋根　　　　Roof　　　　　　　　　　　　56
   欄間　　　　Decorative Transom　　　　　58
   鞘の間　　　Sheath Room　　　　　　　　59
   はとば　　　Hatoba　　　　　　　　　　　60

第 2 章　柔らかな境界
Chapter. 2　　　Soft Boundaries　　　　61

   暖簾　　　　Curtains　　　　　　　　　　　62
   簾　　　　　Blinds　　　　　　　　　　　　64
   襖　　　　　Sliding Solid Doors　　　　　　68
   障子　　　　Sliding Paper Doors　　　　　　70
   屏風・衝立　Folding Screens / Single-Panel Screens　74

第3章　聖と俗、ハレとケの境界
Chapter. 3　　　Sacred and Profane, Ceremonial and Ordinary Boundaries　　　77

床	Alcove	78
神棚	Shinto Altar	79
枝折戸	Wicket Door	80
躙口	Teahouse Entrance	81
茶室	Tearoom	82
沓脱石	Shoe-removing Stone	84
飛び石(露地)	Stepping Stone	86
御手洗	Purification	88
手水	Water Basin	90
鳥居	Shinto Gateway	92
注連縄	Ritual Shinto Rope	96
階段	Stairs	98
白砂壇	Byakusadan	102

第4章　「見立て」の境界
Chapter. 4　　　Simulated Boundaries　　　105

関守石	Barrier Stone	106
みせ	Portable Railing	107
石碑	Stone Stele	109

第5章　風景の中の境界
Chapter. 5　　　Scenic Boundaries　　　111

橋	Bridge	112
坪庭	Pocket Garden	116
借景	Borrowed Landscape	118

第6章　現代の境界
Chapter. 6　　　Contemporary Boundaries　　　121

根津美術館	NEZU MUSEUN	122
House N		128
KAIT 工房	KAIT workshop	135

指定文化財・史跡一覧
Designated Cultural Properties and Historical Sites　　　140

日本的な「関係性の建築」の時代へ

隈 研吾

　実際のところ、今やっと近代建築というものがはじまったのではないかと、僕は感じている。近代建築とは、境界を自由にコントロールできる建築のことであり、境界をコントロールするということは、人と人、人と物、人と自然の関係を繊細にコントロールし、調整することのできる建築である。形としての自分を主張するだけの、自己中心的な彫刻的建築ではなく、様々な関係性のコントロールのために存在する、関係の建築、調整型の建築のことである。

　教科書的にいえば、近代建築＝モダン・アーキテクチュアが生まれたのは、20世紀初頭ということになっていて、異論をはさむ人はあまりいない。その生みの親として名が挙がるのは、フランスのル・コルビュジエ（1887-1965）、ドイツのミース・ファン・デル・ローエ（1886-1969）、アメリカのフランク・ロイド・ライト（1867-1959）の3人であり、近代建築の3巨匠と呼びならわされている。その20世紀初頭の近代建築の特徴は大きくいって2つある。ひとつは装飾のない純粋で幾何学的な形態（白いトウフと思えばいい）、2つ目は内部と外部の透明性であり、わかりやすくいえば壁が少なくなってガラスが多くなったことである。

　その時代に、なぜそういう特徴を持つ建築が生ま

Toward a Japanese-Style Architecture of Relationships

Kengo Kuma

As a matter of fact, I feel that modern architecture has only now, at long last, begun. By "modern architecture" I mean an architecture that can control boundaries at will, that is, an architecture that can subtly adjust relationships between human beings, between human beings and things, and between human beings and nature. It is not a self-centered, sculptural architecture that is formally self-assertive but an architecture of relationships—a regulating architecture that exists to control diverse relationships.

　　　The conventional wisdom is that modern architecture was born in the early twentieth century. Three men, widely referred to as the masters of modern architecture, are credited as its creators: Le Corbusier (1887–1965) of France, Mies van der Rohe (1886–1969) of Germany and Frank Lloyd Wright (1867–1959) of the United States. Modern architecture in the early twentieth century had two distinguishing characteristics. One was pure, unadorned, geometrical forms—imagine buildings resembling white *tofu* —and the other was interior and exterior transparency, which, simply put, meant buildings with few walls and an abundance of glass.

　　　There are mainly two theories as to why an architecture with such characteristics was born in that period. The first identifies society as the root cause. An open society emerged in the twentieth century in place of a closed society, that is, a society divided by various boundaries. According to this theory, in a society without boundaries, architecture has no need of

れたのかについては大別して2説がある。ひとつの説は、原因を社会に求める。閉じた社会、すなわち様々な境界によって仕切られていた社会にかわって、開かれた社会が20世紀に出現した。境界のない社会の建築は、境界（壁）を必要としないという説である。血縁、地縁はじめ、様々な境界がたしかにこの時代に崩壊した。さらにこの開かれた社会からは、装飾も消えていった。なぜなら装飾というのは閉じた社会の色々な約束事を、形態に翻訳したものだからである。たとえば花の模様が柱に刻んであったら、それは女性的なものを象徴していて、その建築は女性的な用途—たとえば女性の寝室—に使われるといったふうな約束事が前提にあって、はじめて装飾が意味を持つ。そういう微妙な約束事で支えられた閉じた社会がなくなれば、装飾という一種の暗号もまた必要なくなるというのが、この説の理屈である。閉じた社会＝暗号の社会＝装飾の社会だったわけである。

2つ目の説は、原因を社会に求めるのではなく、建築の作り方に求める。20世紀に工業化が本格的にはじまり、建築も職人がひとつずつ手で作る時代は終わり、工場で大量生産した部品を現場でアセンブリーする時代がはじまったというのが、この説の論拠である。そういう大量生産システムには、装飾のような余分でごちゃごちゃしたものは不向きだし、石を1個ずつ手で積み上げて作るそれまでの「壁」の建築にかわって、工場で作った鉄とガラスを組み立てて作る、透明で軽やかな建築のほうが適していた、とこの説は主張するのである。

どちらの説が正しいだろうか。しかし、正直なところ、この2つの説ともかなり怪しいと僕は思っている。たしかに20世紀のはじめには、この2つの

boundaries (i.e. walls). Various boundaries, beginning with boundaries based on kinship and region, were indeed destroyed in that period. Furthermore, ornament also disappeared from this open society, because ornamentation was a translation into form of various conventions of a closed society. Ornament takes on meaning only when premised on convention. For example, a floral pattern carved on a column symbolizes femininity and is used in architecture to signify a feminine function, such as a woman's bedroom. This theory argues that if the closed society on which such subtle conventions are based disappears, then there is no longer any need for the form of code called ornament. A closed society = a society of codes = a society of ornamentation.

According to a second theory, the root cause for the birth of modern architecture was not society but the way architecture was made. This theory argues that industrialization began in earnest in the twentieth century; architecture was no longer something to be created by individual craftsmen but a thing to be assembled on the site from parts mass-produced in factories. It asserts that superfluous odds and ends such as ornament were not suited to a system of mass production. A transparent, lightweight architecture made by assembling factory-made steel and glass was more appropriate to such a system than an architecture made by piling stone one by one.

Which theory is correct? Frankly, I find both highly suspect. Admittedly both were persuasive at the start of the twentieth century. At any rate, boundaries in society, beginning with boundaries based on kinship and region, were breached—the closed society was destroyed—with almost frightening speed. Industrialization was so powerful it swept away hand-made systems of craftsmanship. It was unreasonable

説ともかなりの説得力を持っていた。なにしろ恐ろしいほどの勢いで、地縁、血縁をはじめとする社会の境界が崩れ、閉じた社会が崩壊した。工業化も、職人がものを作る手づくりのシステムを一掃する勢いがあった。そんな状況の中で冷静でいろというのが、そもそも無理な話である。冷静ではない頭で、20世紀初頭の建築家は「壁」を捨て、うちそろって透明でトウフのような、「近代建築」へとなだれをうったのである。しかし今、冷静になって考えてみると、当時の近代建築を支えていた2つの理屈は、どちらも疑問だらけである。まず工業化。たしかに20世紀とは工業化の時代だったが、工業化したから透明なガラスの建築にしなければいけないわけではない。壁を多用した工業化だって充分に可能であったわけだし、装飾にしても、決して工業化と対立するものではない。今日の洗練された工業技術をもってすれば、工業化によって、より安く、より美しく装飾を作るなんていうことは、なんでもない話なのである。工業化イコール、境界のない透明な建築というわけにはいかないのである。

境界のない社会という話も、今日の冷静な頭で考えてみれば、かなりマユツバであることがわかる。従来の地縁、血縁にしばられた閉じた社会は、20世紀の到来によって徹底的に破壊された。しかし、だからといって完全に社会の中の境界が破壊されてしまったわけではない。むしろ社会の中には、工業化や情報化によっては、決して取り去ることのできない境界が存在していることに、われわれは今、気づきつつある。境界があるからこそ、安心して生きていけるわけであるし、ひとりでは生きていけない人間というやわな存在がいる限りは、そこにやわなものを守ってくれる、やさしくて暖かな境界がある

to expect people to remain calm under such circumstances. Architects caught up in the excitement of the early twentieth century all rushed to discard walls and to design white, transparent buildings with pure geometrical forms. However, if we now think about this calmly, we see that the two theories on which modern architecture of the time was based—its two rationales—were both highly questionable. Take industrialization. The twentieth century was certainly the age of industrialization, but industrialization did not make a transparent architecture of glass inevitable. Industrialization could just as well have made abundant use of walls, and industrialization was by no means antithetical to ornament. With today's refined technology, creating cheaper and more beautiful ornament through industrialization would be easy. Industrialization does not make a boundary-free, transparent architecture inevitable.

Examined dispassionately today, the idea of a society without boundaries too invites skepticism. The closed society of the past, constrained by boundaries based on kinship and region, was thoroughly destroyed with the arrival of the twentieth century. That does not mean, however, all boundaries in society were destroyed. Instead, we are coming to realize today that there are boundaries that can never be removed by industrialization or advances in telecommunications. We are able to live in comfort precisely because certain boundaries exist. As long as we human beings—fragile creatures unable to live in total solitude and isolation—exist, gentle, flexible boundaries that protect us will survive. Boundaries are not disappearing but instead simply changing form in various ways. To admit we are social beings is tantamount to saying boundaries will not vanish from the world.

Seen in that light, the modern architecture of

のである。境界は残存している。というよりむしろ、境界は消滅しつつあるわけではなく、ただ様々に形を変えているだけであり、われわれがひとりではなく、社会的存在であるということと、世の中から境界がなくならないということは、ほとんど同義といってもいい。人間という社会的存在がいる限り、境界はなくならないのである。

そういう目で眺めてみると、20世紀の近代建築はあまりに乱暴であった。境界がなくなる社会を勝手に仮定して、壁を否定し、装飾をすべて否定してしまったからである。そんな乱暴な建築の中に、そもそもこんなやわな人間が住めるわけがない。

「和」を発想源に再デザインされた境界

歴史をもう少し丁寧に見返してみれば、そもそも20世紀の近代建築のすべてが、それほど乱暴であったわけではない。3人の巨匠が、近代建築の歴史を作ったといわれている。その中で最も境界に対して意識的であったのは、3人の中で最も年長のフランク・ロイド・ライトであった。重たく厚い壁を壊し、内部との境界を壊そうと最初に試みたのはライトである。プレーリー・スタイル（草原様式）＊図1・注1と呼ばれる、大きな屋根と、大きな開口部を持つ透明な建築によって、ライトは20世紀初頭の建築界に衝撃を与えた。もうひとりの巨匠ミース・ファン・デル・ローエはライトの影響のもとに、ユニバーサル・スペース＊注2と名づけられた、さらに透明で壁のない建築を提案した。コルビュジエもまた、ライトの透明性から多くを学び、近代建築の5原則＊注3宣言したのである。ライトは2人に先行し、全くもって独創的であったが、この独創にも実はヒン

＊図1
三層で構成される典型的なプレーリー・ハウスの建築様式

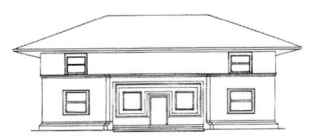

Figure 1
A typical Prairie House composed of three layers.

the twentieth century was much too crude. It rashly postulated a society without boundaries and rejected walls and ornament. We human beings are much too fragile to be able to live in such crude buildings.

Redesigned Boundaries Inspired by Japan

If we look more closely at history, we see that not all works of modern architecture of the twentieth century were crude. Of the three masters said to have written the history of modern architecture, the oldest, Frank Lloyd Wright, was most aware of boundaries. Wright was the first to try to destroy thick, heavy walls and the boundaries between the inside and outside of buildings. His works in the so-called Prairie Style[i] (fig. 1)—transparent buildings with large roofs and large windows—had an enormous impact on the architectural world in the early twentieth century. Under his influence, Mies van der Rohe proposed an architecture of even greater transparency and fewer walls called "universal space."[ii] Corbusier too learned a great deal from Wright's transparency and used what he learned to formulate his own so-called Five Points of modern architecture.[iii] Wright was a highly original architect and anticipated the work of the other two masters, but he did get inspiration from a particular source.

That source was the traditional architecture of Japan. Wright was once an ordinary American architect designing commonplace box-shaped buildings with small windows. However, in 1893 he had a fateful encounter. In that year, the World's Columbian Exposition, commemorating the 400th anniversary of Columbus's landing on the American continent, was held in Chicago. The Japanese government sent carpenters to Chicago to construct a pavilion modeled on the Hoo-do (Phoenix Hall) of Byodo-in (fig. 2). The

トがあったのである。そのヒントとは、驚くべきことに、なんと日本の伝統建築だったのである。1893年以前のライトは、ごくありきたりの、窓の小さな箱型建築をデザインする、どこにでもいる普通のアメリカの建築家であった。しかし1893年以降の彼は、突如として普通のアメリカの建築家ではなくなった。ひとつの建築との出会いが、彼を決定的に変えてしまった。1893年、シカゴでコロンブスのアメリカ大陸発見400年を記念する万国博覧会（世界コロンビア博覧会）が開かれた。日本政府はわざわざ日本から大工をシカゴに派遣し、平等院鳳凰堂を模して日本館*図2を建設した。大屋根が作る大きな影の中の、壁のない透明な建築。他のパビリオンは当時アメリカで流行していたギリシャ・ローマ風の重たく荘重なデザインに染め上げられていたが、日本館だけは決定的に異質であった。大きな屋根の下に、開かれた空間が広がる日本館は、庭園と建築とが一体となり、ギリシャ・ローマ風の重たい建築とは決定的に異なる新しい時代の到来を予感させたのである。この建築との出会いによって、ライトは突如として別人になった。それまでの彼をしばっていた、閉じた箱は開放された。彼は大きな屋根を作り、その下に、透明な空間を展開しはじめたのである。それこそがアメリカの大草原にふさわしい建築だとライトは確信した。そのスタイルをプレーリー・スタイルと名づけ、その開かれた建築様式によって、20世紀建築の幕が落とされたのである。ライトは突如として、建築界の革命家として世界にデビューした。

ただし、プレーリー・スタイルは単に開かれているというわけではない。これは、ライトがプレーリーのモデルとした日本の伝統的建築にしろ同じで

*図2
日本館鳳凰殿正面／出典：『フランク・ロイド・ライトと日本文化』（鹿島出版会）

Figure 2
Front elevation of the Japanese pavilion, the Ho-o-den; from *Frank Lloyd Wright and Japan*

pavilion had a large roof that cast shadows in which transparent spaces without walls were deployed. The building was entirely different from other exposition pavilions, which were heavy, imposing structures in the Greco-Roman style then popular in the United States. The Japanese pavilion, with its open spaces arranged under a large roof, was integrated with a garden and seemed to augur the coming of an architecture very different from the heavy buildings in the Greco-Roman style. After that encounter, Wright became a different architect. He opened up the closed box that had constrained him. He began to create large roofs and to develop transparent spaces underneath those roofs. Wright was convinced that such an architecture was appropriate for the American prairie. He called the style the Prairie Style, and that open architectural style ushered in twentieth-century architecture. Wright suddenly made his world debut as an architectural revolutionary.

However, the Prairie Style was more than merely open, and the same can be said of the traditional Japanese architecture on which the Prairie Style was modeled. Underneath the roof, diverse domains were organized and diverse, subtle boundaries were generated. Various screens were arranged under that roof, subtly separating and connecting domains. Boundaries did not disappear but instead became more evolved. Various boundaries were formed, not just by vertical elements such as walls and screens, but by horizontal elements such as roofs and canopies. Wright learned this technique from Japanese architecture. Boundaries of diverse types and strengths were generated under that large shadow. Wright not only created an open architecture; he became a master of boundaries.

Twentieth-century architects and architectural

ある。屋根はその下に様々な領域を構成し、様々に微妙な境界を生成する。その屋根の下には、様々なスクリーンが配置され、領域と領域とを微妙に仕切り、つないでいく。境界は消滅するどころではなく、むしろ深化した。そして屋根や庇もそれ自体で、境界を形成する建築的装置であった。壁やスクリーンのような垂直のエレメントだけでなく、床や屋根といった水平のエレメントも様々な境界を形成するのである。ライトはその技を日本建築から学んだ。様々な種類と強度を持つ境界が、その大きな影の下に生み出されるのである。ライトは開かれた建築を生み出したのと同時に、境界の名人ともなった。

ライトが好んだこの屋根とスクリーンとを、20世紀の建築家や建築史家は、ライトの後進性と見なした。ライトはその片足を19世紀につっこんでいて、それゆえに屋根やスクリーンから抜け出せなかったのだと彼らは批判したのである。

しかし、当のライトはそんなケチな了見で屋根やスクリーンを用いたわけではない。世界から境界がなくなるわけではないことを、彼ほど理解していた建築家はいない。壁のような乱暴で重たい境界ではなく、格子や障子のような、やわらかな境界、あるいは地面に置かれたひとつの石ころによってほのめかされるような繊細な境界で、世界が再構成されるであろうことが、ライトにははっきりと見えていたのである。

近代建築家がインスパイアされた和の諸要素

それを彼はシカゴの日本館から、安藤広重の浮世絵＊図3・注4から、岡倉天心の『茶の本』＊注5から学んだのである。広重、天心、茶室。それらがライ

＊図3
歌川広重『大はしあたけの夕立』（名所江戸百景）

Figure 3
Hiroshige: *Evening Shower at Atake and the Great Bridge*, from *One Hundred Famous Views of Edo*.

historians saw Wright's love of roofs and screens as evidence of his backwardness. They criticized him as someone who could not free himself from roofs and screens because he still had one foot in the nineteenth century.

However, Wright did not use roofs and screens because he was unsophisticated. More than any other architect, he understood that boundaries were not going to disappear from the world. He saw clearly that the world was likely to be reorganized not by crude, heavy boundaries such as walls, but by soft boundaries such as louvers and *shoji* screens and subtle boundaries suggested, for example, by the placement of a single stone upon the ground.

A Modern Architect's Japanese Inspiration

Wright learned these truths from the ukiyo-e prints of Ando Hiroshige[iv] (fig. 3) and *The Book of Tea* by Kakuzo Okakura.[v] Hiroshige, Okakura, and the tea house suggested to Wright a mature civilization, and the mature spaces distinctive to it. Wright's encounter with the transparent spaces based on multilayered boundaries achieved in Hiroshige's ukiyo-e prints enabled him to go beyond the perspectival space of the West. He was able to transcend the laws of perspective to express depth in space that had constrained Western architecture and painting since the Renaissance. Hiroshige had as powerful an impact on Wright as the Japanese pavilion at the Chicago Exposition. Just as Hiroshige expressed depth in woodblock prints by overlapping various screens (i.e. boundaries) in two dimensions, Wright expressed depth in buildings by overlapping screens in three dimensions.

The Book of Tea, written in English and published in the United States in 1906, was also a

トに示したものは、ひとつの文明の成熟であった。文明の成熟に特有の、成熟した空間であった。広重が浮世絵の中に実現した、境界の重層性にもとづく透明な空間との出会いによって、ライトは西洋の遠近法的空間を超越したといわれる。ルネッサンス以来の西洋の建築と絵画とをしばっていた遠近法による奥行きの表現を、彼はついに超越したのだ。シカゴ万博の日本館と同じような衝撃を、広重はライトに与えた。広重が様々なスクリーン（境界）を重ねていくことで空間の奥行きを表現したように、ライトもまたスクリーンで建築物に奥行きを与えていった。

英語で書かれ、アメリカで1906年に出版された『茶の本』も、ライトに圧倒的な影響を与えた。天心は、茶室の本質は、その実体の中にあるわけではなく、その実体の中に生成された空（くう）の中にこそあるのだと看破した。ただし建築を実体としてとらえるのではなく、その実体の中に生成される空間としてとらえる考え方は、天心の独創ではない。19世紀、ドイツを代表する建築家、ゴットフリート・ゼンパー（1803-1879）は、このような「空」の建築論、すなわち形態的建築観にかわる空間的建築観のパイオニアといわれ、形態的・実体的建築論を否定した彼の考え方の延長に、空間の流動性、透明性をテーマとする近代建築運動がはじまったとされる。すなわち、ライト、ミースという系譜の原点はゼンパーの空間的建築論だと近代建築史は整理される。しかしライトは、ゼンパーの理論の影響を受けたというより、天心の『茶の本』から直接的に、空間的な建築表現を獲得したのである。『茶の本』との出会いは、ライトにとって衝撃的であり、彼の人生と作品にとって、シカゴの日本館との出会いと同

major influence on Wright. Okakura saw that the essence of a tea house lay not in the building itself but in the void generated in that building. The idea that architecture is not a material object but the space generated inside that object was not original, however, to Okakura. Gottfried Semper (1803–79), a representative German architect of the nineteenth century, is regarded as the first to develop such an architectural theory of space, that is, a spatial view of architecture as opposed to a formal view of architecture. The modern architecture movement, with its themes of spatial continuity and transparency, is said to have started as an extension of Semper's rejection of a formal, material theory of architecture. That is, modern architectural history declares that the starting point for the architectural line of development represented by Wright and Mies was Semper's theory of architectural space. Rather than being influenced by Semper's theory, however, Wright obtained his idea of space directly from Okakura's *The Book of Tea*. His encounter with *The Book of Tea* had a great impact on Wright and was as important to him as his encounters with the Japanese pavilion and Hiroshige's ukiyo-e prints. He himself said, in a 1954 lecture at the University of Oklahoma: "In it [*The Book of Tea*] I read this—the reality of the building does not consist of the four walls and the roof but in the space to be lived in! . . . I came down like a sail coming down. . . . Why . . . after all . . . 500 years before Jesus—Lao-tse! What to do now? Where to go from here? I couldn't destroy the book. . . . I mean . . . I knew I couldn't hide! I knew the damned thing had to come out!"[vi]

Late in life, Wright was almost too candid, all but admitting that the spatial view of architecture which was a basic principle of the tea house had given birth to his architecture and triggered the

じょうに、広重との出会いと同じように決定的であった。彼自身こう記している。

「その（茶の本）中に私は次の文を見つけた。建物の全体は4つの壁と屋根にあるのではなく、生活する空間に存在するのである！　私は船の帆が下りるように座り込んだ。いったい、なぜ―キリストよりも500年も前の―老子なのであろう。これからどうすればよいのだろう。ここからどこに行けばよいのだろう。本を切り刻んでしまうことはできなかった。つまり、それを隠すことができないことはわかっていた。このいまいましいものが世に出るべきであることを知っていたのだ」(1954年のオクラホマ大学のレクチャーより)。

茶室の基本原理ともいえる空間的建築観が、直接的に彼の建築を生み出し、彼が創始した近代建築の引き金となったことを、晩年のライトはあまりにも正直に告白しているのである。

文化円熟期としての「近代」の再来

ひとつの新しいテクノロジーは、社会を決定的に変質させる。新しいテクノロジーは、従来の社会を分割していた境界を破壊する。すべてのテクノロジーとは、本来そのような性質を持っている。その意味でのテクノロジーとは暴力であり、野蛮である。しかし、社会は破壊されたままでいることはできない。いったん破壊された社会は、新たに再編された境界を用いて再生を試みるのである。境界の破壊というフェーズが終了し、ゆったりと少しずつ境界が再構築される。この状態がすなわち文明の成熟である。この状態こそが近代という状態なのである。近代とは時代のことではなく、ひとつの状態である。

emergence of modern architecture.

Modernity as a Recurring Condition of Cultural Maturity

A new technology can cause a decisive transformation of society. A new technology can destroy the boundaries that divide society. All technologies have such a capacity. In that sense, technology is violent and barbaric. However, society cannot remain in a state of destruction. A society that has been destroyed tries to revive itself using newly reorganized boundaries. The phase in which boundaries are destroyed comes to an end, and gradually, boundaries are reconstructed. That is how a civilization attains maturity. That condition of maturity is what is called "modernity." Modernity refers not to a period in history but to a condition. Modernity does not refer merely to the early twentieth century. When a new technology has ended its period of growth and vitality and passed its peak, the reorganization of boundaries begins. The reorganization restores to people a place where they can feel comfortable and regain their equanimity.

It was not an accident that Japan provided the best model for the condition called modernity. Japan did not produce new technologies on its own but was buffeted for centuries by new technologies introduced from China. It was always the passive receiver of new technologies. How was society to recover from the impact of a new technology? How was the equilibrium of daily life to be restored after the destructive impact of a new technology? This small country always focused its energy on solving those questions. Japan was always desperate to achieve the condition of maturity called modernity. However, that does not mean that Japanese culture lacked originality and was

近代とは20世紀初頭だけをさすわけではない。ひとつの新しいテクノロジーが、イケイケの時期を終え、そのピークを過ぎた時に、境界の再編成がはじまり、境界の再編成によって、人々はもう一度居場所を取り戻し、落ち着きを取り戻そうとするのである。その状態が、近代である。

その近代という状態の最良のモデルが日本にあったのは、決して偶然ではない。日本は自ら新しいテクノロジーを生み出すのではなく、隣人の中国からもたらされる新しいテクノロジーに翻弄され続けた。新しいテクノロジーに対して絶えず受身であり、受動的であった。新しいテクノロジーの衝撃をどうリカバーするか。その破壊的衝撃のあとで、いかに日々の安らかな生活を再構築するかに、この小さな国は全力を注いできたのである。近代という成熟した状態を獲得するために、絶えず必死だったのである。だからといって、この国の文化が中国のコピーであり、独創的ではないというわけではない。むしろこの国の文化は徹底して独創的であった。衝撃を緩和して、社会を再編成するという目的のために、この国は極めて独創的な文化をはぐくんできたのである。その文化の中心にあったのが、境界という概念であり、境界をたくみにデザインすることによって、破壊を修復することに、安らかな生活を取り戻すことに、この国の能力は発揮されたのである。その産物が広重であり、天心であり、茶室であった。それらが一貫してめざした状態が、一言でいえば近代という状態だったのである。

だから近代というものは何度でも訪れる。ひとつの国が何度も何度も近代を体験する。日本に限った話ではない。ギボン*注6が描いたローマ帝国の衰退の中にも近代があり、ホイジンガ*注7が示した『中

---

merely a copy of China. Rather, Japanese culture was thoroughly original. Japan nurtured an extremely original culture in order to ease the impact of new technologies and to facilitate the reorganization of society. At the heart of that culture was a concept called boundaries, and it was in the skillful design of boundaries intended to repair what had been destroyed and restore tranquility to life that Japan demonstrated its particular genius. The ukiyo-e prints of Hiroshige, the ideas of Okakura, and the tea house were all products intended to achieve the condition called modernity.

    Modernity can therefore occur any number of times. A country can experience modernity any number of times. This is not something limited just to Japan. There was modernity in the decline of the Roman Empire described by Gibbon,[vii] and there was a different modernity in the "autumn of the Middle Ages" depicted by Huizinga.[viii] These historians used the words "decline" and "autumn" to give beautiful expression to that condition. Japan definitely experienced modernity in the Heian period, the Muromachi period and the Edo period. It experienced modernity each time a new technology matured and a kind of stagnation began to prevail. Japan is a country that for geographical reasons cannot help but assume a passive stance with respect to newly introduced technology, whether it likes it or not; it has had no choice but to experience modernity numerous times. Wright, the possessor of a rare sensibility, recognized the subtle boundaries that had developed as a result in this country.

    Modernity is another name for refinement in the technique of boundaries. Today, we have been made painfully aware of that fact—an awareness that accounts for publications such as this very book.

世の秋』もまた、ひとつの近代であった。彼らはそれを「衰退」とか「秋」という言葉を使って美しく表現したのである。そして平安時代にも、室町にも、江戸にも、近代はまぎれもなく存在したのである。新しいテクノロジーが円熟し、一種の停滞が訪れるたびにわれわれは近代を体験してきたのである。とりわけ日本という、好むと好まざるとにかかわらず地勢的に、新たに輸入されたテクノロジーに対して受動的にならざるをえないポジションにある国は、頻繁に近代を体験せざるをえない。そこに出現した繊細なる境界群に、ライトというたぐいまれなる感性が注目したのである。

言い方を変えれば、近代とはすなわち境界技術の洗練の別名なのである。今日、われわれはそれを痛感している。痛感しているから、このような本の出版が企画されたのだろう。工業化という新しいテクノロジーが円熟し、時をおかずして、情報化という新しいテクノロジーもまたたく間に円熟期を迎えた。しかし、境界が消えたわけではない。消えるどころではない。新しい種類の新しい性能を持った、様々な境界が生まれつつあり、それらの新しい境界が、文明の成熟を美しくいろどるのである。

それゆえに今、日本建築が輝くのである。日本建築は、境界の技術の宝庫であり、イケイケの終わった時代を生き抜くための知恵が、日本建築の中に満載されている。様々なスクリーン〔たとえばルーバー（格子）や暖簾（のれん）や、様々な中間領域（縁側・廊下・庇（ひさし））〕が環境と建築とをつなぐ装置として再び注目されている。地球環境問題に関心が集まり、サステナブル（接続可能）なデザインが注目される今、これらの建築装置は、サステナブルデザインの先例としても注目を浴びているのである。それらは太陽光をカッ

Industrialization, once a new technology, reached full development; now, the technology called telecommunications is very quickly entering its stage of full development as well. However, boundaries have not disappeared. Boundaries are not about to disappear. New types of boundaries with new capabilities are coming into being, and the new boundaries are lending color to the maturity of civilization.

That is why Japanese architecture is now so splendid. Japanese architecture is a treasure-trove of boundary techniques, and is full of ideas for surviving an age in which growth has ended. Diverse screens (such as louvers and *noren*) and intermediate domains (such as verandas, corridors and eaves) are gaining attention once more as devices for connecting the environment to buildings. Today, when the focus is on global environmental issues, these architectural devices are of great interest as precedents for sustainable design. They enabled people in the past to dwell at high density in places with limited supplies of energy and resources while screening off sunlight, promoting ventilation, and controlling security. As the entire global environment deteriorates, the design of boundaries that developed under the special conditions prevailing in Japan cannot help but attract the interest of the rest of the world. The entire world can be said to be undergoing Japanization, and this Japanization of the environment is demanding Japanese design. As a result, Japanese design is to be found at different scales and in different guises in leading-edge architectural projects throughout the world. Though most Japanese themselves are still unaware of what is happening, the world is thus being Japanized.

Bruno Taut (1880–1938), the German avant-garde architect, visited Japan in 1933 and suddenly burst into tears at the sight of a bamboo fence at

15

トし、通風を可能にし、セキュリティーを調整しながら、エネルギーも資源もない場所で、人々が高密度に暮らしていくことを可能にしてくれていたのである。すなわち、日本という特殊な条件の中で育てられてきた境界のデザインが、今この地球環境全体の悪化の中で、注目を浴びざるをえなくなっているのである。地球全体が日本化したといってもいいし、その環境の日本化が、日本のデザインを求めているのである。その結果、日本的デザインがスケール・形を変えながら、世界をリードする建築プロジェクトの中によみがえりつつある。当の日本人が気づかないうちに、世界はそんな形で日本化しつつある。

ドイツの前衛建築家ブルーノ・タウト（1880-1938）は、1933 年に日本を訪れて、桂離宮の竹垣*図4 の前で、突如として泣き崩れた。近代建築のエースと目されていたタウトが、なぜこの古くさい竹垣の前で、なぜこの古びた境界の前で泣き崩れなければな

らないのか。当時の日本人には全く理解ができなかった。当時の日本もまた、20 世紀の新たなテクノロジーによってもたらされた暴力の信奉者でしかなかった。「ヨーロッパの建築家たちは、モダニズムをとなえながら依然として形の世界にいる。形という乱暴な世界の中にいる。一方、日本の建築家たちは、はるか数世紀の前から、関係の世界を生きてきた」とタウトは痛感し、『日本美の再発見』という名著を残した。日本建築の繊細さを引き合いにしながら、その庭と建築との微妙な関係に驚嘆しながら、彼はコルビュジエやミースの暴力を批判するのである。タウトは日本を訪れる前、鉄に熱狂し、ガラスに熱狂し、それらの新しいテクノロジーをテーマにして建築を作った。新しい技術への熱狂において、彼の右にでる建築家はいない。しかし激しい熱狂があったからこそ、彼は、その直後、決定的に醒めざるをえなかったのである。関係という複雑で微

*図 4
桂離宮 桂垣（宮内庁京都事務所）

Figure 4
Bamboo fence, Katsura Detached Palace (Kyoto Office, Imperial Household Agency)

Katsura Detached Palace (fig. 4). What was it about the old-fashioned bamboo fence, the antiquated boundary, that reduced a leading figure of modern architecture to tears? The Japanese of the time could not understand it. They believed, like many other countries, in the violence caused by new technology in the twentieth century. "European architects remain in a world of forms, even as they advocate modernism. They remain in a violent world called form. On the other hand, Japanese architects have lived for centuries in a world of relationships." Those words are from Taut's great book, *Nihonbi no saihakken* (Rediscovery of Japanese Beauty). Critical of the violence of Corbusier and Mies, he cited the delicacy of Japanese architecture and expressed admiration for the subtle relationships between Japanese gardens and buildings. Before visiting Japan, Taut had been excited about steel and glass and had created buildings with these materials as

their theme. There was no architect as enthusiastic about these new technologies as Taut. However, in Japan he suddenly awakened, as from a dream. He began delving into the complex and subtle world of relationships. A world of relationships is a world in which there is an awareness of boundaries—a world that is gentle to human beings. In the bamboo veranda of Katsura Detached Palace, in the subtle integration of its garden and architecture, Taut discovered a culture of relationships, a culture of boundaries. He could not help but burst into tears in front of the bamboo fence. The Japanese of the time did not understand the meaning of his tears.

We Japanese are already sick and tired of new technologies. Of course new technologies will emerge in the future in different products and in different guises, and people may from time to time become enamored of those new technologies. What of it? We

妙な世界へと、踏み込まざるをえなかったのである。関係の世界とは、すなわち境界に対して意識的な世界のことであり、人間に対して徹底してやさしい世界の別名である。タウトは桂離宮の竹の縁側に、その庭と建築との絶妙な融合の中に、関係性の文化、境界の文化を発見したのである。そして竹垣の前で泣き崩れざるをえなかった。当時の日本人は、その涙の意味するところが、わからなかった。

　すべての新しいテクノロジーというものに、われわれはすでに飽き飽きしているのである。もちろんこれからも様々なテクノロジーが品を変え形を変えて出現し、人々はその新しいテクノロジーに対してたびたび熱狂するかもしれない。しかし、それがどうしたというのだろうか。そのような熱狂を超越した境地にわれわれは達しつつある。大切なのは、テクノロジーへの熱狂ではなく、そのテクノロジーを使い倒すことであり、そのテクノロジーを退屈に感じることであり、そのテクノロジーの暴力から、世界をねばり強く修復することである。その優雅な退屈が日本建築を生み出したわけであり、その退屈が、様々な境界技術を生み、そして育ててきたのである。退屈を恐れてはいけない。退屈こそ豊かさの母であり、豊かな建築の母に他ならないのである。

are approaching a condition that transcends such enthusiasms. Enthusiasm over technology is unimportant. What is important is using a technology until it has nothing new to show us, reaching a stage where that technology can only fill us with boredom, and patiently repairing the damage inflicted on the world by the violence of that technology. An elegant ennui gave birth to Japanese architecture; boredom produced and nurtured diverse boundary techniques. We must not be afraid of boredom. Boredom is the mother of invention; boredom is the mother of an inventive architecture.

Endnotes

*注1
プレーリー・スタイル
大地を覆うように低く設置された屋根と仕切り壁をなくした広い室内空間を擁する、プレーリー・ハウス（草原住宅）と呼ばれるライトの建築様式。

*注2
ユニバーサル・スペース
モダニズム建築の理念のひとつで、いかなる用途にも適応するように、特に目的を定めない空間のこと。壁や柱を最小限に抑え、必要に応じて間仕切りの位置や家具の位置を変化させることで、自由で可変的な利用を可能とした。建築家ミース・ファン・デル・ローエが提唱。

*注3
近代建築の5原則
壁ではなく柱を主な構造体とする建築を推進し、壁の占める面積を減らすことによって生まれた自由度の高いデザインを生かすべく、コルビュジエが提唱した近代建築の理念。建物を柱で支え、地下階に吹き抜けを設ける「ピロティ」、水平な屋上に設置する「屋上庭園」、壁による仕切りをなくしたことにより生じる「自由な平面」、広い開口で高い採光性を確保する「横長の窓（水平連続窓）」、構造体に壁を用いることからの脱却により生じた「自由なファザード」の5点が挙げられる。

*注4
安藤広重の浮世絵
歌川（安藤）広重（うたがわ ひろしげ）〈1797~1858〉は江戸時代の浮世絵師。『東都名所』『東海道五十三次』など、叙情的で親しみやすい画風が人気を集め、風景画家として葛飾北斎とならんで確固たる地位を築いた。『名所江戸百景』は広重最晩年の連作浮世絵。大胆な構図や鮮やかな色づかいで、同時代から後のヨーロッパでみられた日本趣味の指向「ジャポニズム」に対して多大な影響を与えた。

*注5
岡倉天心の『茶の本』
岡倉天心（おかくら てんしん）〈1863~1913〉は明治期の美術史家、美術評論家、美術教育者。本名は覚三（かくぞう）。東京美術学校（現・東京藝術大学）の設立に大きく貢献し、日本美術院の創設者としても著名。『茶の本』は1906年初版発行。

*注6
ギボン
エドワード・ギボン（1737~1794）。イギリスの歴史家。古代ローマ帝国の最盛期から東ローマ帝国の滅亡までを記した歴史書『ローマ帝国衰亡史』（1776）の著者として知られる。

*注7
ホイジンガ
ヨハン・ホイジンガ（1872~1945）。オランダの歴史家。主要著書は、14~15世紀のブルゴーニュ公国の生活・思想・芸術の諸形態を描いた『中世の秋』（1919）、「遊び」を人間の本質的文化活動とした『ホモ・ルーデンス』（1938）など。

[i] An architectural style developed by Frank Lloyd Wright distinguished by a low roof that hovers just over the earth and extended interior spaces free of partitions.

[ii] One of the ideals of modernist architecture—a space without any predetermined function that can be adapted to any use. Limiting walls and columns to a minimum and changing the locations of partitions and furniture as necessary made it possible to freely change the way space was used. Proposed by the architect Mies van der Rohe.

[iii] The principles of modern architecture proposed by Corbusier. Designs that assure a high degree of freedom were to be achieved by making columns rather than walls the main structure and thus reducing the overall area of walls. The five points were "pilotis," an unenclosed area at ground level created by raising the building on pillars, a "roof garden" created on a flat roof, a "free plan" created by eliminating the use of walls for partitions, "horizontal windows" with large areas of glazing that assure an abundance of daylight, and a "free façade," made possible by freeing walls from a structural function.

[iv] An atmospheric, accessible style in works such as *Famous Places in the Eastern Capital* and *Fifty-Three Stations of the Tokaido Road*, made ukiyo-e artist Utagawa (Ando) Hiroshige (1797–1858) popular, and he, like Katsushika Hokusai, earned a reputation as a landscape artist. *One Hundred Famous Views of Edo* was a series of ukiyo-e from his final years. With its bold compositions and fresh use of colors, it was responsible in part for the rise of japonisme, the influence of Japanese taste on European culture around this time.

[v] Kakuzo Okakura (1863-1913) was an art historian, critic and educator of the Meiji period. Better known by his pen name, Tenshin Okakura, he played a major role in the establishment of Tokyo School of Fine Arts (the present-day Tokyo University of the Arts) and is also known as the founder of Japan Fine Arts Academy.

[vi] From Kevin Nute, *Frank Lloyd Wright and Japan*, London, 1993.

[vii] English historian Edward Gibbon (1737–94) is the author of *The History of the Decline and Fall of the Roman Empire*, recording the history of the empire from its zenith to the fall of the East Roman Empire.

[vii] Dutch historian Huizinga's main works are *The Autumn of the Middle Ages* (also translated as *The Waning of the Middle Ages*), which depicts the forms of life, philosophy and art in the Burgundian court in the 14th and 15th centuries, and *Homo Ludens*, which posits "play" as humanity's essential cultural activity.

第1章　内と外の曖昧な境界

Vague Boundaries Between Interior and Exterior

　言葉によって世界を切り取り認識しやすくするのと同様に、人は「自己の側」に属する空間を形成するために、仕切りや標といった「境界」を用いてきた。

　すると必然的に、自己の側以外の空間は、混沌とした「外部」空間に位置づけられる。人はしばしば、高い障壁などの強固な境界により、カオス＝外部を拒絶した。「内と外」の二元論によって、世界を整理した。

　しかし実際のところ、人間とは外部＝自然環境との関連性によって生かされているにすぎない生物で、そのようなデジタルな処理では対応しきれない、もっと複雑で矛盾をはらむ生身の存在だということに、この国の人々は早くから気づいていた。

　そして、外部との関係性を完全には断ち切らない、さまざまな「境界」が発展した。

Just as we use language to parse reality to make it more easily apprehensible, we employ boundaries—parsings of space—and conventional signs in order to give comprehensible form to the space around us. As an inevitable result of this process, the space other than that around us is assigned an identity as the amorphous "outside." People have frequently tried to keep the outside, the chaos, at bay by building high walls and impregnable boundaries. They categorized the world according to the dualism of inside and outside. But in fact, our species cannot survive if it rejects its interrelatedness to the "outside"—that is, our natural environment—and the people of Japan long ago perceived that that we are a more complex and contradictory organism than the simple digital operation of 1 or 0, "either–or" can explain. This is how many different kinds of boundaries that do not completely separate outside and inside came to exist in Japan.

窓

Mado
Window

採光・通気・開放性の獲得以外の、日本の窓の仕事。
室内に生じる明暗に、等しく価値を与えること。
外部に拡がる無限の世界を想像させること。

In addition to providing light, ventilation, and a feeling of openness, in Japan windows enhance interior light and shadow equally and evoke the infinite space of the world outside.

旧春日大社板倉　円窓亭（奈良市高畑町）
Former Kasuga Shrine Wooden Storehouse
(Takabatake-cho, Nara)

杉本家住宅（京都市下京区）
Sugimoto Residence (Shimogyo-ku, Kyoto)

「火袋」と呼ばれる台所の吹き抜け天井に設置された採光用の窓。
Windows set in the upper level of the two-story open area over the kitchen.

森村家住宅 円窓（奈良県橿原市）
Morimura Residence (Kashihara, Nara Prefecture)
Window panel with rounded corners.

窓
Mado
Window

林家住宅（長野県木曾郡南木曾町）
Hayashi Residence (Nagisomachi, Kiso-gun, Nagano Prefecture)

蔀戸

Shitomido
Hinged Shutter

障子戸が生まれる以前から、日本人を風雨から守っていた建具。
外部との接続は、戸を跳ね上げて確保する。

The *shitomido* is a large shutter hinged at the top, used to protect the interior from wind and rain before the invention of sliding wooden doors. Access to the exterior is created by propping or hanging the shutter open.

坂野家住宅（茨城県常総市）
Sakano Residence (Joso, Ibaraki Prefecture)

草野家住宅（大分県日田市）
Kusano Residence (Hita, Oita Prefecture)

格子組の裏に板を張った建具で、日光を遮り、風雨を防ぐ。多くは上下2枚に分かれ、下1枚は立てたまま、上は建物本体に金物で吊り、室内側または室外側へ水平に跳ね上げて採光・通気する。

The *shitomido* consists of a lattice framework to which boards are attached. It keeps out both light and inclement weather. Most *shitomido* consist of a set of two panels divided horizontally. The lower panel remain vertical and the upper one is attached to the building with a hinge, so that it can be lifted, either toward the interior or the exterior, to provide light and ventilation.

格子

Koshi
Lattice

通行人に対しては、
その軽やかなピッチによって圧迫感を軽減し、
住人に対しては、
適度に遮蔽してプライバシーを保ちつつ、同時に光と風と音を取り入れる。
内と外、双方への配慮が生んだ、日本建築の代名詞的存在。

For passersby, the open texture of the lattice ameliorates the oppressive feeling of a solid wall, and for the resident, it provides a degree of privacy and protection while allowing light, air, and sound into the interior. The lattice structure is one of the most characteristic features of traditional Japanese architecture, born from a consideration of both interior and exterior.

吉島家住宅 (岐阜県高山市)
Yoshijima Residence (Takayama, Gifu Prefecture)

江戸期の「揚屋建築」の唯一の遺構。「揚屋」とは現在の料理屋・料亭にあたる。座敷・調度・庭などにおいて社寺の書院・客殿と同等のしつらえがなされた、京都における民間最大規模の饗宴の場であった。

角屋（京都市下京区）
Sumiya (Shimogyo-ku, Kyoto)

The only remaining example of *ageya*-style architecture from the Edo period. The *ageya* is equivalent to a modern exclusive restaurant. Its rooms, furnishings, and gardens employed the designs and décor of the *shoin* and *kyakuden* (types of reception or guest halls) of temple architecture and provided the largest and most luxurious entertainment facilities for the citizens of Kyoto.

犬矢来

Inuyarai
Protective Screen

仰々しさのないこの「柔らかな魔よけ」が、
都市のファサードを形成していた。

These unimposing, "soft barriers" are an important feature of traditional urban streetscapes.

岐阜県高山市
Takayama, Gifu Prefecture

公道に面した町家外壁に置かれるアーチ状の垣根。短期間での使用を前提とし、
竹や木などでできたものが多い。泥よけ、犬や猫の小便防止、外壁保護の役割を果たす。

An *inuyarai* is a concave screen placed along the boundary walls of buildings facing the street. Since they require regular replacement, they are made of common materials such as bamboo or wood strips. They protect the building from mud and fouling or damage by animals or people.

垣根

Kakine
Fence or Hedge

嵯峨野 竹林（京都市右京区）
Sagano Bamboo grove (Ukyo-ku, Kyoto)

乗り越えようと思ったら、簡単に乗り越えられる。
その抑制は、見る者の良識に委ねられる。
仮設性の強い、意識に「待った」をかけるためのまじない。

Not so tall as to prevent climbing over, the effectiveness of a fence or hedge relies upon the good will of others. Temporary structures often of light, natural, or living materials, they are a kind of gentle reminder to halt and go no farther.

堅固とはいいがたい垣を強力な結界たらしめるのは、その清浄さが
魔を防ぐと信じられてきた青葉の力である。

生け垣（京都市右京区）
Hedge (Ukyo-ku, Kyoto)

Though far from impenetrable, a hedge is regarded as establishing a firm boundary because of its greenery, which was traditionally regarded to keep demons out through its purity.

シベリア颪は、冬は寒気団をともなって日本海沿岸に雪を降らせ、雪の降らない時期には強風を運んでくる。村民自らの手でつくるこの柵は、海岸からの強風に運ばれてくる飛砂や吹雪を防ぐための自衛手段である。

Cold air masses from Siberia drop heavy snows on the areas along the coast of the Japan Sea and bring powerful winds. This fence, built by the villagers, is a means of protection from the sand, gravel, and blizzards accompanying those winds.

折林の柵（秋田県由利本荘市）
Fence in Oribayashi (Yurihonjo, Akita Prefecture)

垣根

Kakine
Fence or Hedge

高温多湿に加え、台風などの自然災害に対し、沖縄では様々な工夫がなされている。防風林である福木を密に植え、珊瑚石の石垣をめぐらし、家屋に直接風があたらないようにしている。福木の葉は肉厚で塩風にも火にも強く、塩害・防火の役割も果たしている。

In addition to tropical temperatures and humidity, Okinawa is buffeted by frequent typhoons and other extreme weather patterns. Garcinia is planted as a windbreak, and coral rock used to protect the home from powerful winds. The leaves of the garcinia are thick and resistant to fire and salt, providing extra protection from both manmade disasters and the elements.

福木と珊瑚石の塀（沖縄県島尻郡伊是名村）
Fence of *fukugi* (*Garcinia subelliptica*, common garcinia, a kind of mangosteen) and coral rock. (Izena-mura, Shimajiri-gun, Okinawa Prefecture)

塀

Hei
Wall

安藤家住宅（山梨県南アルプス市）
Ando Residence (Minami Arupusu, Yamanashi Prefecture)

出雲大社本殿 外塀（島根県出雲市）
Izumo Shrine Main Hall Outer fence (Izumo, Shimane Prefecture)

外敵を防ぎ、自己の領域を確保するための原初的な境目。
堅固なものや可視性・装飾性の高いもの、
その様々な形状は、「境」に対する人々の意識の高さの表れか。

The most primeval form of boundary, to keep intruders out and protect one's space. The various forms that walls take—from formidable to visually appealing and decorative—may be an expression of their attitude toward boundaries.

門

Mon
Gate

石畳の階段を上がり一段高くなった山門を潜ると、初めて伽藍が目に入る。ここで光景は一変し別世界、仏域に導かれる。山門手前の石碑には「不許葷辛酒肉入山門」と刻まれている。「葷」は臭いの強いニンニクなどを指し、食した者の入山を許さない。

法然院 山門 (京都市左京区)
Hōnen'in Sanmon (Sakyo-ku, Kyoto)

Climbing up the stone steps and then passing through the Sanmon Gate atop them, one sees the temple for the first time. At this point the vista is transformed into another world, and one is led into the realm of the Buddha. The stone monument before the gate is engraved with the words, "Those Who Have Partaken of Pungent or Hot Foods, Alcohol, or Meat May Not Enter."

元来堅固につくられるべきであるにもかかわらず、
垣根も塀も併設されない、
また物理的抑制力の乏しい簡素な門が、この国には数多く存在する。
人の意識に抑制を促す「結界」として、
それで十分に役割を果たせるからである。

Though one would expect gates to be sturdily built, there are many gates in Japan that are quite simple in design and construction, physically unimposing, and not attached to fences or walls. That's because they're able to function as a sign that communicates the message of a boundary or passageway.

上江洲家住宅（沖縄県島尻郡久米島町）
Uezu Residence (Kumejima-cho, Shimajiri-gun, Okinawa Prefecture)

薩摩藩内に113あった外城(藩の支配制度による区分の呼称)のひとつである入来麓。麓とは戦国時代にはじまった武家屋敷群で、軍防を目的とした街造りである。外敵に備えて閉鎖的な武家門や茅葺門の多い中、イヌマキの木をそのまま刈り込んでできた開放的な植木の門は珍しい。

Satsumasendai is the modern name of Iriefumoto, one of the 113 administrative units of the Satsuma fief known as *tojo*. A *fumoto* was an enclave of samurai residences first established in the Warring States Period, forming a town as a defensive unit. It contained many gates that served as defensive measures—among which this less formidable topiary podocarpus gate would have been a relative rarity.

植木門 (鹿児島県薩摩川内市入来町麓)
Topiary Gate (Satsumasendai, Kagoshima Prefecture)

門

Mon
Gate

門扉のない沖縄の民家の門から入ると、正面に「ひんぷん」と呼ばれる目隠しの塀がある。これは入口から直接建物の内部が見えないよう造られたもので、中国伝来の魔除けの塀が沖縄で独自に発展したものである。

銘苅家住宅（沖縄県島尻郡伊是名村）
Mekaru Residence (Izena-mura, Shimajiri-gun, Okinawa Prefecture)

The gateway to a traditional Okinawan house has no doors, but a wall called the *hinpun* stands behind the open entryway to prevent those at the entryway from seeing directly into the home. This is a unique Okinawan version of the "demon-blocking wall" in traditional Chinese homes.

玄関

Genkan
Entrance

渡辺家住宅（千葉県夷隅郡大多喜町）
Watanabe Residence (Otakimachi, Isumi-gun, Chiba Prefecture)

「バリアフリー」という聞こえのよい言葉で
画一化された空間とは一線を画す。
通過時に身体に負担を強いるほどの段差。
身体がそう感じるからこそ、意識にも確かな変化が刻まれる。

A space of a different order from so-called "barrier-free," homogenized, uniform space. A change in spatial quality distinctive enough to make its presence firmly felt as you pass through. The physical sense of moving from one zone to another awaken the mind to a shift in mental attitude as well.

江川家住宅（静岡県伊豆の国市）
Egawa Residence (Izunokuni, Shizuoka Prefecture)

土間・三和土

Doma/Tataki
Earth or Mortar Floored Areas

江川家住宅（静岡県伊豆の国市）
Egawa Residence (Izunokuni, Shizuoka Prefecture)

玄関であり、貴重な生産作業の場であり、
時には共同体の集会所にもなる。
公的な外部空間と、私的な家族空間のちょうど中間に位置する場。
屋内の土を「汚い」と捉える現代的な感覚が、
不遜である気がしてしまう。

An entrance, a place where important tasks are carried out, and sometimes even the locale for community gatherings. A zone precisely situated between public, exterior space and private, interior space. Our modern view of earth inside the home being "dirty" seems somehow disrespectful.

江川家住宅（静岡県伊豆の国市）
Egawa Residence (Izunokuni, Shizuoka Prefecture)

松延家住宅（福岡県八女郡立花町）
Matsunobu Residence (Tachibanamachi, Yame-gun, Fukuoka Prefecture)

土間・三和土

Doma/Tataki
Earth or Mortar Floored Areas

我妻家住宅（宮城県刈田郡蔵王町）
Wagatsuma Residence (Zaomachi, Katta-gun, Miyagi Prefecture)

家の中で、床を張らず地面のまま、または三和土（たたき）になった所。三和土とは床面の土に粘土と石灰と苦汁（にがり）を混ぜ、板や棒で叩いて締め固めたもの。

An area in the home with a floor of exposed earth or pounded mortar. Pounded mortar floors are made by pounding a mixture of clay, charcoal, and brine spread over exposed earth with boards and timbers.

通り庭

Tori-niwa
Open Corridor

光が通り、音が通り、風が通る。
家の内部に設けられた外部空間。

An exterior space bringing light, sound, and air into the home's interior.

旧中村家住宅（岩手県盛岡市）
Former Nakamura Residence (Morioka, Iwate Prefecture)

吉田家住宅（京都市中京区）
Yoshida Residence (Nakagyo-ku, Kyoto)

町家などにおいて、表入り口から裏口へ通り抜けのできる土間。上部は天窓付きの広い吹き抜けにされ、風の通り道にするとともに直射日光を防ぎ、夏期の室温の上昇を抑制する。

The tori-niwa is an earthen-floored corridor that leads from the front to the rear entrance of the home in the urban residential architecture known as *machiya*. It has skylights and high ceilings. The tori-niwa creates cross ventilation and, because it is roofed over, it helps keep the house cool in the summer.

縁側

Engawa
Veranda

虫の音、日だまり、中秋の名月。
北風、豪雨、底冷えの雪。
恩恵と苦難、双方をそのまま受け入れる姿勢。
飼い慣らす気など毛頭ない、
自然への畏敬の念が表出する場所。

The cries of insects, sunbeams, the beautiful moon of autumn.
The north wind, driving rain, the coldness of snow on the ground.
Accepting blessings and adversity equally, just as they are.
A place where one experiences the awe of nature,
untamed.

渡邉家住宅（新潟県岩船郡関川村）
Watanabe Residence (Sekikawa-mura, Iwafune-gun, Niigata Prefecture)

日本家屋で、建物の縁に張り出して設けられた板敷きの部分。玄関以外の出入り口を兼ねる。

In the traditional Japanese house, this is a board-floored area projecting from the perimeter of the house, also serving as an entrance, in addition to the genkan entryway.

渡邉家住宅（新潟県岩船郡関川村）
Watanabe Residence (Sekikawa-mura, Iwafune-gun, Niigata Prefecture)

縁側
Engawa
Veranda

旧奈良家住宅（秋田県秋田市）
Former Nara Residence (Akita, Akita Prefecture)

縁側

Engawa
Veranda

旧内山家住宅（富山県富山市）
Former Uchiyama Residence (Toyama, Toyama Prefecture)

軒

Noki
Eaves

内部でもあって外部でもあり、
しかしそのどちらでもないグレー・ゾーン。
明確な仕切りのない、境界とも呼びがたい境界。

Both outside and inside, but at the same time a gray zone that is neither. A boundary without any clear division, hard even to call a boundary.

林家住宅（長野県木曾郡南木曾町）
Hayashi Residence (Nagisomachi, Kiso-gun, Nagano Prefecture)

屋根の下端の、建物の外部に差し出たところ。庇。

Noki are the eaves that project over the external walls of the house.

軒

Noki
Eaves

知覧麓庭園 森家（鹿児島県南九州市）
Chiran Fumoto Park, Mori Residence (Minami Kyushu, Kagoshima Prefecture)

壁

Kabe
Wall

この世の住処は、所詮かりそめの宿。
日本人が元来共有していた住居観を代弁するかのような、
はかない茅の壁。

Our dwellings in the world are merely temporary.
A wall made from rushes, representing the traditional Japanese view of the home as an evanescent thing.

かつてこの住宅が所在していた秋山郷は、信濃と越後の国境、山深い豪雪地帯である。屋根が茅で葺かれているばかりでなく、壁も茅を竹で押さえて段葺きとし、家全体が茅で包まれている。屋内も大部分が茅壁である。

旧山田家住宅（大阪府豊中市）
Former Yamada Residence (Toyonaka, Osaka Metropolitan District)

This residence was formerly located in the Akiyama district on the border of Shinano and Echigo provinces, an area with deep winter snows. Not only does it have a rush-thatched roof, but the walls are made of layers of rushes held in place by bamboo strips, so that the entire dwelling is blanketed in rushes. Most of the interior walls are the same.

屋根

Yane
Roof

苔むした茅葺き屋根（京都府南丹市）
A rush-thatched roof covered with moss (Nantan, Kyoto Metropolitan District)

境界を生成するのは、
壁や戸といった垂直のエレメントだけではない。
水平のエレメントである屋根もまた、
その傘下につくられる境界によって、
多様な質を備えた空間を生成する。

Vertical elements such as walls and doors are not the only way to create interior boundaries in a house. The roof, a horizontal element, can create space of a rich variety of qualities, through the boundaries resulting from the spaces it encloses.

この地方としては珍しく、正面軒下に装飾のための関西風の格子が取り付けられている。障子戸と合わせ、250年以上前に建てられた古くからの養蚕農家の美しさを一層引き立たせている。

Rare for this part of Japan, this house has decorative lattice in a style more common in Western Japan beneath the eaves. Together with the sliding doors, they highlight the beauty of this home, built more than a quarter-century ago, where silkworms were cultured.

旧新井家住宅　板葺き石置き屋根（埼玉県秩父郡長瀞町）
Former Arai Residence Rush-thatched roof with stone weights (Nagatoro-cho, Chichibu-gun, Saitama Prefecture)

欄間

Ranma
Decorative Transom

開かれた場所に設置されれば、
その存在によって、連続する空間が意識の上で線引きされる。
閉じられた場所に設置されれば、
その透過性によって、線引きされた空間に連続性が与えられる。

When installed in an open area, the decorative transom softly divides space in the viewer's mind.
Installed between two separated spaces, it links them through its semi-open structure.

熊谷家住宅（山口県萩市）
Kumaya Residence (Hagi, Yamaguchi Prefecture)

天井と鴨居との間に、採光・通風・装飾のために、竹の節・格子・透かし彫り彫刻の板などを取り付けてある部分。

A ranma is a decorative transom installed between the ceiling and a lintel. It provides light and ventilation and is often decorative, with woven bamboo strips, latticework, or relief carvings set within its framework.

鞘の間

Sayanoma
Sheath Room

縁側のさらに内側にある「緩衝地帯」。
日本建築の境界線は、グラデーションで成り立っている。

A narrow interior space adjacent to the *engawa* that serves as a "buffer zone."
The boundaries in Japanese architecture have a range of gradations.

縁側のように細長い部屋。また、本堂と鞘堂（本体を保存するため、それを覆うように建てた建築物）との間にある細長い空間。

The *sayanoma* (literally, "sheath room") is a long narrow space with *tatami* flooring, or a long narrow space between a precious main building and a building built over it *(sayado)* as a protective covering

旧笹川家住宅（新潟市南区）
Former Sasagawa Residence (Minami-ku, Niigata, Niigata Prefecture)

はとば

Hatoba

川を引き込み、屋内に取り込む。
生活者の率直な欲求が具現化したこのようなものにこそ、
自然＝外部を拒絶対象とは見なさない、
日本人古来の考え方の原形が表れる。

Bringing a stream into the house. This is the realization of a prototype of the ancient Japanese impulse to embrace the outside, Nature, rather than distance oneself from it.

藍場川の水を屋敷内に引き入れ、流水式の池水庭園を造っている。池を出た水は家の中に造られた「台所はとば」で家庭用水として使われた後、再び藍場川に戻される。

Water from the Aiba River is drawn into the house to create a flowing water garden. After the water running out of the pond is drawn from the *hatoba* (literally, a dock or waterfront, but here a landing to access the water by descending a stairway) in the kitchen it is once again returned to the river.

旧湯川家（山口県萩市）
Former Yukawa Residence (Hagi, Yamaguchi Prefecture)

第 2 章　柔らかな境界

Soft Boundaries

布・紙・竹、
およそ物理的抑制力など無いに等しい素材で、
可視性のみを損なわせる。
つながりつつも、区切りたい。
そういう一見矛盾した願望をかなえさせる装置たち。

Fabric, paper, bamboo
Materials that actually provide almost no physical protection,
but merely restrict possibilities.
Joining and separating at the same time.
Furnishings that accomplish two apparently contradictory
functions at once.

暖簾

Noren
Curtains

角屋（京都市下京区）
Sumiya (Shimogyo-ku, Kyoto)

通過の際、頭を下げず、手を使わない人は稀である。
わずかでも頭をかしずかせ、手を使わせる「弱い力」が、
思いのほか強い力となって、人に空間の質の違いを認識させる。

Very few people pass through a curtain without dipping their heads or parting the panels with their hands. The gentle motions of inclining the head or brushing aside the cloth is surprisingly amplified and makes us aware that we are passing into a space of a different quality.

縄暖簾
Rope *noren*

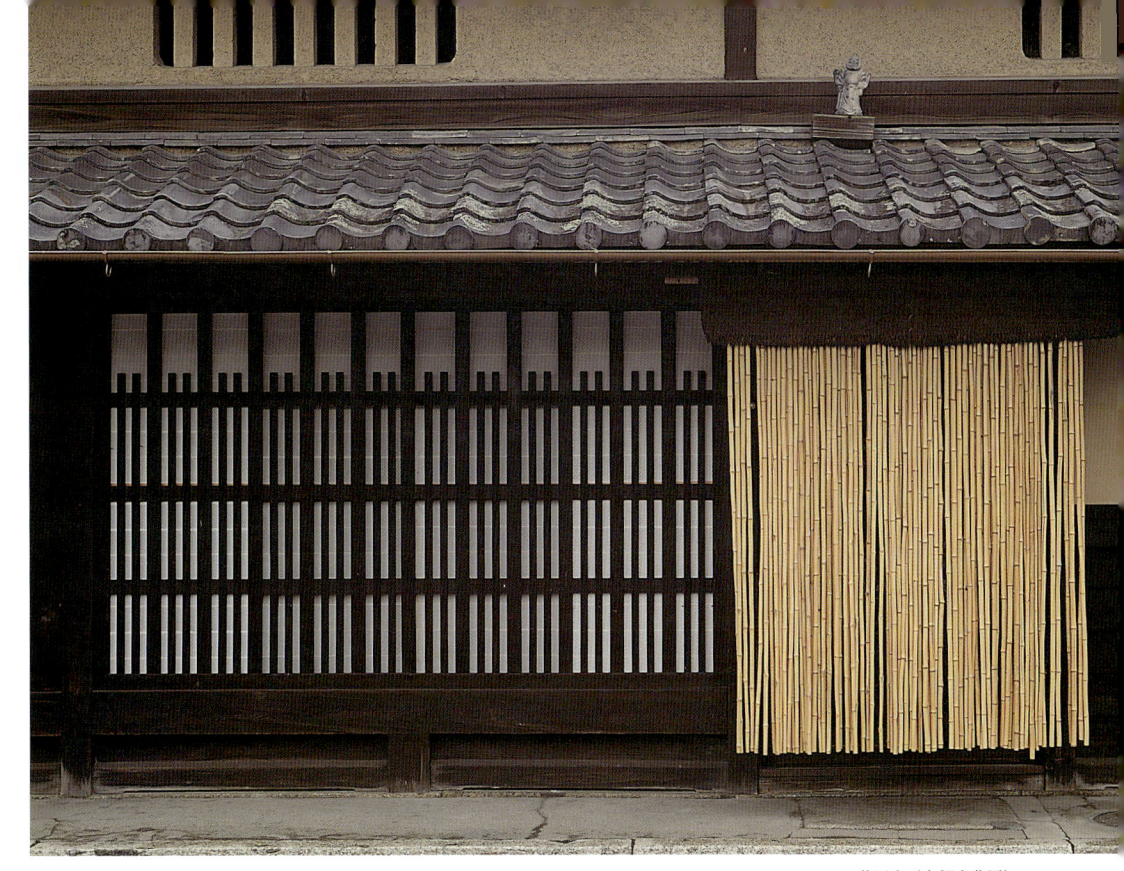

荒川家（京都市北区）
Arakawa Residence (Kita-ku, Kyoto)

主に布で作られ、軒先に掛け日よけ・目隠しとする。商家では、屋号（称号）を染めて看板ともした。縄や竹で作られたものもある。

Most *noren* are made from cloth and hung from the eaves to provide shade and privacy. From the Edo period, merchants has their trademarks printed on *noren*, and they became a kind of logo. *Noren* are also made of rope and bamboo.

太田家（秋田県仙北市角館町）
Ota Residence (Kakunodatemachi, Senboku, Akita Prefecture)

簾

Sudare
Blinds

簾の「す」という言葉には、
「隙」「透」という意も込められている。
それ故か時折感じさせられる、
ガラス以上の透明性。

The *su* of *sudare* is related to the words for "gap" and "transparent."
Perhaps that's why at times they sometimes seem more transparent than glass.

細い蘆、または細竹を編み連ね、日よけなどの目的で垂らすもの。

Sudare are blinds woven from thin reeds or bamboo sticks and hung for protection from the sun or for privacy.

ぎをん萬養軒（京都市東山区）
Gion Man'yoken (Higashiyama-ku, Kyoto)

喜多家住宅（石川県石川郡野々市町）
Kita Residence (Nonoichimachi, Ishikawa-gun, Ishikawa Prefecture)

大角家住宅（滋賀県栗東市）
Osumi Residence (Ritto, Shiga Prefecture)

簾

Sudare
Blinds

吉田家住宅（京都市中京区）
Yoshida Residence (Nakagyo-ku, Kyoto)

襖

Fusuma
Sliding Solid Doors

那須家住宅（宮崎県東臼杵郡椎葉村）
Nasu Residence (Shiiba-mura, Usuki-gun, Miyazaki Prefecture)

優れた調湿機能を備えた、
設置の自由度の高い仕切り戸。
夏の快適さ＝通風性を第一としていた、
日本家屋の必需品である。

Providing insulation and allowing for flexible placement, *fusuma* also offer good ventilation for summer comfort, making them an indispensable element of the Japanese house.

馬場家住宅（長野県松本市）
Baba Residence (Matsumoto, Nagano Prefecture)

平安時代の日本で発祥した建具。木組の心材に和紙を下張りし、その上に襖紙を張り、椽（ふち）と引手を付けて仕上げる。生活の都合や季節の変化、儀礼などに応じて、屏風や障子などと共に内部を仕切り、その都度適切な空間演出を行った。

Fusuma developed in the Heian period. They consist of a wood framework over which Japanese paper is applied. Another layer of special *fusuma* paper is applied over that, and edging and indented handles attached. Resting in tracks set into the floor below and lintels above, they can be moved or removed, and in combination with sliding paper doors *(shoji)* and folding screens *(byobu)* can be used to divide or open the interior space in many different ways in response to the needs of daily life, the seasons, or ceremonial occasions.

障子

Shoji
Sliding Paper Doors

温かく、柔らかく、思いのほか強い和紙という素材。
まるで「神宮式年遷宮」のように、
定期的な張り替えという「再生」が、終末の到来を遠ざける。

The warm, soft, yet surprisingly strong material of Japanese paper *(washi)*. Continually renewed—like the regular rebuilding of famous shrines—by repapering, shoji can last a long time.

復古館頼家住宅（広島県竹原市）
Fukkokan Rai Residence (Takehara, Hiroshima Prefecture)

今西家書院（奈良市福智院町）
Imanishi Residence (Fukuchiin-cho, Nara)

間仕切りとして、また家屋の扉や開口部などに用いる建具の総称。広義には襖・衝立なども含まれる。現在では多く、中世以降発達した「明障子」のことを指す。

Shoji is a general term for the furnishing used as dividers and doors throughout the Japanese house. Broadly speaking, it also includes *fusuma* and *tsuitate* (single-panel screens), but today the term generally refers to the *akari shoji* (light-transmitting siding doors) that came into use in Japan's medieval period.

旧黒澤家住宅（群馬県多野郡上野村）
Former Kurosawa Residence (Ueno-mura, Tano-gun, Gunma Prefecture)

障子

Shoji
Sliding Paper Doors

富澤家住宅（群馬県吾妻郡中之条町）
Tomizawa Residence (Nakanojomachi, Agatsuma-gun, Gunma Prefecture)

屏風・衝立

Byobu/Tsuitate
Folding Screens / Single-Panel Screens

たとえば室内の片隅に設置し、
その影でもてなしの下準備をする場をしつらえることで生じる、
即席の異空間。
高い装飾性を誇る、空間を自在に操る調度品。

Placing a screen in the corner of a room, one can create a special place for making the preparations for entertaining a guest, instantly transforming the space.
Screens are both highly decorative and make it possible to manipulate space freely.

復古館頼家住宅（広島県竹原市）
Fukkokan Rai Residence (Takehara, Hiroshima Prefecture)

屏風
室内に立て風よけ・仕切・装飾などとして用いる具。木枠の上に紙や絹を貼ったものをつなぎ合わせ折り畳めるようにしたもの。

Byobu, or folding screens, are decorative furnishings used to provide protection from drafts and divide interior space. They consist of paper or silk affixed to wood frames, and the individual panels are hinged to allow them to be folded and to stand freely.

衝立
一枚の屏障具に台を取り付け、どこにでも設置可能にしたもの。

A *tsuitate* is a single-panel screen that is set in a low stand to hold it upright and allow it to be placed freely within the interior.

堀家住宅（奈良県五条市）
Hori Residence (Gojo, Nara Prefecture)

屏風・衝立

Byobu/Tsuitate
Folding Screens / Single-Panel Screens

吉村家住宅（大阪府羽曳野市）
Yoshimura Residence (Habikino, Osaka Metropolitan District)

第3章　聖と俗、ハレとケの境界

Sacred and Profane, Ceremonial and Ordinary Boundaries

段差、柱、標など、
人に注意を喚起させる何かによって区切られた聖域。
崇拝と畏怖の対象となる、
人智を超えた存在としての「外部」を
確立させる結界たち。

Different levels, pillars, signs—things such as these are employed to mark off sacred space. These are the boundaries that delineate the outer as an object of worship and awe, transcending human knowledge.

床

Toko
Alcove

旧矢掛本陣石井家住宅 上段の間（岡山県小田郡矢掛町）
Kyuyagake Honjin Ishii Residence Formal reception room (Yagakemachi, Oda-gun, Okayama Prefecture)

わずかな段差と飾り柱などのしつらえが、
その場に最上級の格付けを行う、
最大限の讃辞であるかのようだ。

A minor difference in level and a decorative pillar make the *toko* a place of honor, conferring the highest praises upon it.

座敷飾りの一。ハレの空間である間の一角に作られ、掛け軸や花などを飾る場。

One of the decorative features of a room. A special alcove in which decorative scrolls or flowers are displayed. Also called the *tokonoma*.

神棚

Kamidana
Shinto Altar

家の中に設けられる最上級のハレの空間。
周囲より少しでも高くするのは、
人間心理として、ごく自然な行いかもしれない。

The most hallowed place in the home.
It is perhaps only natural that people should try to make it a little higher than the surrounding space.

建物の中で、神符を収め、神道の神を祭る祭壇。

An altar architecturally incorporated into the house where Shinto talismans are enshrined and Shinto gods worshiped.

旧目黒家住宅（新潟県魚沼市）
Former Meguro Residence (Uonuma, Niigata Prefecture)

枝折戸

Shiorido
Wicket Door

成人の腰の高さにも満たないほど、
茶庭の露地の植栽と同化するように佇む、
この小さな門を通過することで、人は禊ぎを行う。
日常と非日常の境。

When you pass through this small gateway, lower than an adult's waist and blending in with the plantings of the roji tea garden, you are engaged in an act of purification.
A boundary between the everyday and the extraordinary.

木の枝を折って作った簡素な戸という意味の、竹や木の枝の框に菱目に竹を組み込んだ戸のこと。主に茶室露地の中門として用いられる。

The word *shiori* means "broken branches," and a *shiorido* is literally a very rough and simple gate made from broken branches. It has a wood or bamboo frame with bamboo strips woven in a crosshatched pattern. It is usually used as the middle gate in the roji (tea garden) leading up to a *chashitsu* (tearoom).

紫織庵〈川﨑家住宅〉（京都市中京区）
Shiroi-an [Kawasaki Residence] (Nakagyo-ku, Kyoto)

躙口

Nijiriguchi
Teahouse Entrance

茶室の出入り口。出入りには頭を低くする謙虚な姿勢が求められる、茶の心を体現する扉。標準的な建具の幅は約 65 センチ、高さは約 70 センチ。

The entrance to a teahouse. It's size and placement force those passing through it to lower their heads in a humble posture, thus experiencing the spirit of tea. The standard size for a *nijiriguchi* is 65 centimeters wide by about 70 centimeters high.

法然院 茶室「如意庵」(京都市左京区)
Hōnen'in Tearoom Nyoi-an (Sakyo-ku, Kyoto)

「完全形には発展がない」という考えに基づき、
板 2 枚半という半端な数で構成される戸。
身をかがめて入ることで、
極小の空間に無限の広さが与えられる。

Based on the idea that there is no room for growth in something that's complete, this small door is the size of two and one-half boards, an incomplete measurement.
By forcing visitors to bend low to enter the tearoom, it imparts the tiny space with an infinite expanse.

茶室

Chashitsu
Tearoom

木・土・紙、
有限の資材を用いて生成された、
無限の空(くう)の世界。
この国の空間構成術、そのすべての結晶体。

A realm of infinite emptiness created from the conditioned materials of wood, earth, and paper. The tearoom is the epitome of the Japanese art of spatial design.

茶室 如庵(愛知県犬山市)
Tearoom Jyo-an (Inuyama, Aichi Prefecture)

茶の湯に使うための室。この呼称が定着したのは近代に入ってから。四畳半を広さの基準とし、それ以上を広間、それ以下を小間と呼ぶ。四畳半は両方を兼ねる。

A tearoom *(chashitsu)* is the space were *chanoyu* (the art of tea) takes place. The term only gained widespread use in recent centuries. The standard tearoom is four and one-half *tatami* mats in size.

沓脱石

Kutsunugi-ishi
Shoe-removing Stone

室内に「穢れ」を持ち込まないため、
心に節目をつけるため。
どれだけ西洋化が進んでも、
この国の「家の中では履き物を脱ぐ」習慣だけは失われなかった。

No matter how Westernized Japan has become, the custom of removing one's shoes before entering the house has been preserved, to keep dirt from being carried inside and as a mental marker.

吉田家住宅（京都市中京区）
Yoshida Residence (Nakagyo-ku, Kyoto)

喜多家住宅（石川県石川郡野々市町）
Kita residence (Nonoichimachi, Ishikawa-gun, Ishikawa Prefecture)

草野家住宅（大分県日田市）
Kusano Residence (Hita, Oita Prefecture)

玄関や縁側などの上がり口に、履き物を脱いでおくため、また、昇降しやすいよう置いた石。

A stone set at the entrance or the place where one steps up onto the *engawa* where one can remove one's shoes. Its height also makes the step up easier.

飛び石(露地)

Tobi-ishi
Stepping Stone

石から石へ、移動の儀式。
定められたリズムに律された身体が、
自ずと別世界へと導かれてゆく。

Stepping from stone to stone.
When your progress is defined by the spatial rhythm of the stones,
you are naturally led into a separate realm.

永富家住宅（兵庫県たつの市）
Nagatomi Residence (Tatsuno, Hyogo Prefecture)

法然院（京都市左京区）
Hōnen'in (Sakyo-ku, Kyoto)

庭園・露地で、歩き易さを考慮し、また道標となるべく並べられた石のこと。庭の点景としての美を演出する役割も果たす。

Stepping stones are employed in gardens and along the path in the *roji* (tea garden) to make it easy to walk and also to mark the way. They also contribute to highlighting the especially scenic points in the garden.

御手洗

Mitarashi
Purification

聖域に入る前には、
神官も参拝者も、この場で行水をして、
心身をともに洗い清めるのが儀式の正道であった。

Before entering a sacred precinct, both priests and worshipers wash their hands and purify body and mind in the appropriate ritual.

一の鳥居（参道のもっとも外側の鳥居）をくぐり、そこから奥に進むと五十鈴川のほとりに石畳が敷きつめられている。心身を清めるすがすがしい水辺。石畳は元禄五(1692)年、五代将軍徳川綱吉の生母、桂昌院が寄進したものである。

After passing through the outermost *torii* gate, stone steps lead down to Isuzugawa River on the right. The water's edge is a refreshing locale to purify body and mind. The steps were built in 1692, through a donation from Keishoin, the mother of the fifth Tokugawa Shogun, Tsunayoshi.

神宮内宮 御手洗場（三重県伊勢市）
Ise Shrine Inner Shrine Hand-washing place (Ise, Mie Prefecture)

手水

Chozu
Water Basin

神宮内宮 手水舎（三重県伊勢市）
Ise Shrine Inner Shrine　Hand-washing Shelter　(Ise, Mie Prefecture)

手を洗い、口をすすぐ。
行水に見立てたこの行為により、
人は世俗の塵を払い落とす。

Washing the hands and rinsing the mouth—these acts symbolizing purification remove the dust of the world.

一の鳥居の手前にある。柄杓で左手、右手の順に洗い、残った水を左の掌に受けて、口中を清める。このような所作は神道でいう禊ぎである。そして神域へ。

Located in front of the first *torii* gate to the shrine. One used the dipper to wash first the left hand, then the right, pouring any remaining water into the palm and then using it to rinse the mouth. This is the a form of Shinto purification, after which one can enter the sacred precincts.

吉田家住宅 蹲踞(つくばい) (京都市中京区)
Yoshida Residence Hand-washing basin (Nakagyo-ku, Kyoto)

神社などにおいて参詣者が手や口をすすぎ清める行為である「手水(ちょうず)」。神宮御手洗場 (pp. 88-89) のように、かつては周辺の河川や湧き水で清めを行うのが通例であった。手水はその簡略化されたもの。茶室に入る前にも蹲踞(手水鉢)で身を清める。

Chozu refers to the act of worshipers purifying themselves by washing their hands and rinsing their moths before worshiping at a shrine. As the photograph of Ise Shrine on pp. 88–89 shows, this was originally done at a nearby stream or spring. *Chozu* is an abbreviated form of this ritual. One also purifies one's body and mind before entering the tearoom, at a water basin *(tsukubai* or *chozubachi)*.

鳥居

Torii
Shinto Gateway

その名も形状も、由来は定かではない。
ただ、この標は我々にとって、
「神聖なるもの」を表すサイン以外の何物でもない。

The origins of the name and the form of the Shinto gateway are obscure. This sign, however, is an expression for the Japanese of the sacred.

神宮内宮 宇治橋（三重県伊勢市）
Ise Shrine Inner Shrine Ujibashi (Ise, Mie Prefecture)

神社などにおいて、神域への入口を示す一種の門。左右二本の柱の上に横材（笠木）を渡し、その下に連結するための貫を入れて構成される。

The *torii* is a type of gate used at Shinto shrines and other places to mark the entryway into sacred space. The two vertical pillars of the gate are capped with a lintel and a tie beam.

八幡宮（青森県平川市）
Hachiman Shrine (Hirakawa, Aomori Prefecture)

中央部の太くなった注連縄を掲げるのは東北地方に多く見られる風習である。現在はその結い手も減少傾向にあるという。

Such ropes with a distended center tied to the two pillars of a *torii* gate are frequently seen in the Tohoku region of Japan. The number of individuals who know how to weave them are declining, it is said.

境内は日本海を一望できる高台に位置し、200本余りの赤い鳥居が曲線を描きながら続く。鮮やかな朱色は、生命の躍動を表し、災いを防ぐ意を込め多く鳥居に用いられる色である。

The shrine precincts are on a hill, affording a view of the Japan Sea, and contain more than two hundred red *torii* gates in a curving path. The bright red represents the vitality of life, and, as a kind of charm against misfortune, is the most common color for *torii*.

高山稲荷神社（青森県つがる市）
Takayama Inari Jinja (Tsugaru, Aomori Prefecture)

鳥居
Torii

蚕ノ社〈木嶋坐天照御魂神社〉三つ又鳥居（京都市右京区）
Kaiko no Yashiro (Konoshima-ni-Masu-Amateru-Mitama Jinja) Mitsumata Torii

通称「蚕ノ社」と呼ばれる木嶋神社。本殿の西側に四季湧水する「元糺の池」という池があり、池中に天保2（1831）年に再建された珍しい石製三柱の鳥居が建っている。

Konoshima Shrine, also known as Kaiko no Yashiro. To the west of the main shrine is a spring-fed pond, Motodasu no Ike, and when the shrine was rebuilt in 1832, this rare three-post *torii* was built in it.

注連縄

Shimenawa
Ritual Shinto Rope

木にも鏡にも、何もない空間にも、
囲われたこの場の中に、神が宿る。

A god dwells in the area circumscribed by this sacred Shinto rope, whether a tree, a mirror, or nothing at all.

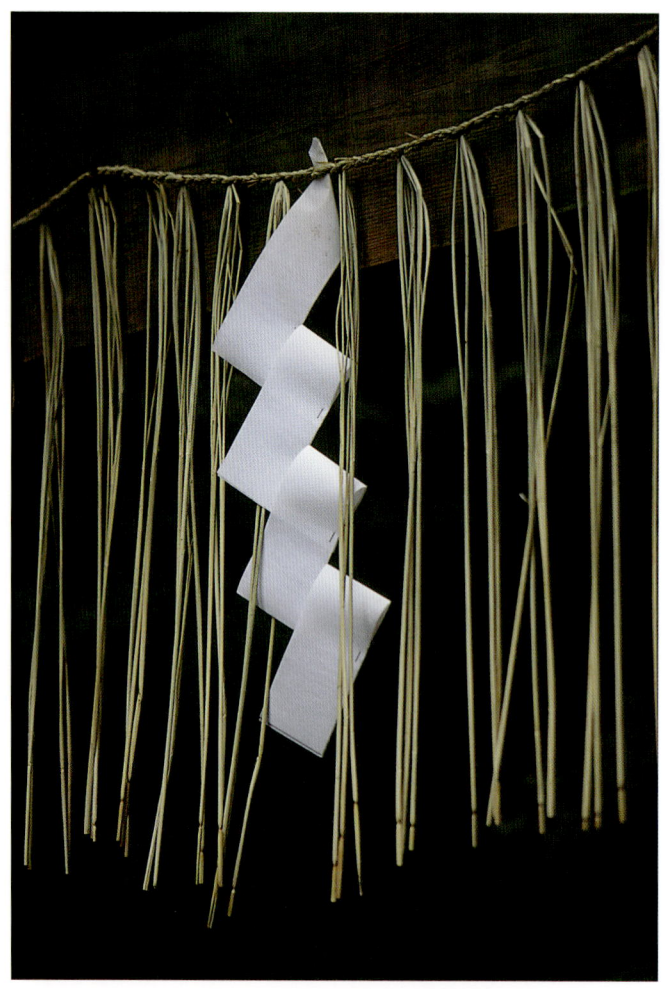

蚕ノ社〈木嶋坐天照御魂神社〉（京都市右京区）
Kaiko no Yashiro (Konoshima-ni-Masu-Amateru-Mitama Jinja)

神前または神域の場に、不浄なものの侵入を防ぐ標として張る縄。

A *shimenawa* is a ritual rope in front of a deity or sacred space that acts as a marker to prevent anything impure from entering the area it demarcates.

江川家住宅 生柱（静岡県伊豆の国市）
Egawa Residence (Izunokuni, Shizuoka Prefecture)

土間境中央の注連縄を張った柱は、柱根があり「生柱」と呼ばれている。現在の建物の前、江戸時代初期寛永 (1624~43) の頃に建てられたときから存在する、江川家の象徴である。

The pillar in the center of the *doma* with the *shimenawa* tied to it has roots, which is why it's called a "living pillar" *(ikebashira)*.

階段

Kaidan
Stairs

神護寺（京都市右京区）
Jingoji (Ukyo-ku, Kyoto)

一段一段を踏みしめる行為そのものが、
聖なる場に近づくためのイニシエーションとなる。

The act of climbing one step at a time is an act of initiation for approaching the sacred space.

神護寺（京都市右京区）
Jingoji (Ukyo-ku, Kyoto)

御正宮へ続く30段余の石段。その高みの奥に正殿が建つ。神宮式年遷宮は、20年に一度、社殿や御装束・神宝のすべてを新しくして、神に新宮へお遷りいただくわが国最大のお祭りである。

The thirty stone steps leading up to the main shrine above. In one of the most important ceremonies in Japan, the shrine, its furnishings, and sacred treasures are replaced with new ones every twenty years, to offer the gods a new shrine.

階段

Kaidan
Stairs

神宮内宮 正宮への石段（三重県伊勢市）
Ise Shrine Inner Shrine Stone steps to the main shrine (Ise, Mie Prefecture)

白砂壇

Byakusadan

法然院（京都市左京区）
Hōnen'in (Sakyo-ku, Kyoto)

白砂壇は、水すなわち池を表している。人は二つの白砂壇の間を通ることで心身を清め、浄域に入ることができる。文様は雨や風でくずれる度に、修行僧の手によって新しいものに描き換えられる。

The piles of white sand represent water, or ponds. Passing between the two piles of white sand, the body and mind are purified and one enters a sacred space. Whenever the patterns of the sand are disturbed by wind or rain, they are refashioned by the temple priests.

第4章 「見立て」の境界

Simulated Boundaries

床に生けた花で野を喚起させたり、
水を用いず山河を表現したり。
ある物を見たときに、
別の物を想起し対応付けることである、
日本人の得意とする「見立て」の手法。
単独では特に意味があると思われない装置たちが、
同じ文化圏に属する人間同士が共有する
「暗黙の了解」を前提として、
人の認識に抑制力を働かせる区切りに見立てられる。

The flowers displayed in the *toko* remind one of flowers growing in the fields; depicting mountain streams without using water. This is the art of simulation at which the Japanese excel—using something to suggest something else. Elements that don't seem to have any special meaning on their own are able, through a silent shared understanding of the members of the same cultural complex, to simulate and suggest boundaries that demand out attention.

関守石

Sekimori-ishi
Barrier Stone

この単なる小さな石が、
大きな抑制力をもたらすサインとなるには、
サインに気付けるだけの「良識」を持ち合わせていることが、
受け取る側に求められる。

For this little stone to act as a potent sign,
the interpreter of the sign needs to share a common awareness
that apprehends and gives it meaning.

法然院（京都市左京区）
Hōnen'in (Sakyo-ku, Kyoto)

茶庭の飛び石や延段の岐路に据えられる、縄で十文字に結んである小石。「これより先は遠慮下さい」との意を示す暗黙の印。

A *sekimori-ishi* is a small stone tied with a rope and placed on a stepping stone in a tea garden or a crossroads of a stone path meaning, "Do not proceed further."

みせ

Mise
Portable Railing

帳簿格子という結界が、向かい合う人々を、
瞬時にして「主」と「客」の役に分けさせる。

The railing in front of a clerk's work area immediately separates shopkeeper from customer.

草野家住宅（大分県日田市）
Kusano Residence (Hita, Oita Prefecture)

室内の一角に構えた店構え。格子で設けた「結界」の中で、番頭が帳簿付けをする「帳場」である。宗教用語から出た「結界」は、商家のなかにあって、主人と決められた者以外決して越えてはならない見えない境界線として存在している。無用の者が入ると厳しく叱責される。

A furnishing typical of traditional shops, placed in one section of the room. The boundary established by the railing creates the area where the head clerk manages the shop's accounts. Instead of a religious boundary, this marks an invisible line beyond which no one but the shopkeeper may enter. Anyone else will receive a harsh rebuke for violating it.

みせ
Mise
Portable Railing

外村宇兵衛邸（滋賀県東近江市）
Tonomura Uhei Residence (Higashiomi, Shiga Prefecture)

石碑

Sekihi
Stone Stele

川のへりに立てられた石碑。
石に刻まれた文字を読まずとも、
その存在が、ここが「結界の要」であることを如実に示している。

A stone stele standing by a riverbank. Even without reading its inscription, its very presence clearly signals that this is the gateway to an important boundary.

神護寺 清滝川（京都市右京区）
Jingoji Kiyotakigawa (Sakyo-ku, Kyoto)

寺に至ろうとすると、短いけれど清滝川に架かる朱塗りの橋、高雄橋を渡らなければならない。この橋のたもとに、中世から近世のある時期まで「女人禁制」であったことを示す「万治3年（1660）造」と刻まれた禁制碑が建っている。

In order to reach the temple, one must cross a short but highly arched red bridge over Kiyotakigawa. At the foot of the bridge stands a stone stele with the inscription "Built in 1660" and "Women Forbidden to Cross" —a rule in effect from the medieval to mid- early modern period.

第5章 風景の中の境界

Scenic Boundaries

観光地でカメラのシャッターを押すときに働いている、
その場を「切り取るべき風景」と捉える主観的かつ
自己中心的な視点。
その瞬間、切り取る自己＝内部は、
切り取られる対象＝外部から隔てられる。
「風景の中の境界」とはその隔たりのことを指すのではなく、
自己の主観が生み出したにすぎない、
そのような錯覚を融解し、
内と外を再接続させる装置のことである。

When you click the shutter of your camera at a tourist spot, you're motivated by a subjective, self-centered feeling that this is something you should try to capture. At that moment, you as the photograph taker (inside) are separated from the object you wish to capture on film (the outside). "Scenic boundaries" does not refer to this separation of subject and object. Rather, it is the mechanism that dissolves the illusion that is merely your subjective creation and reconnects inside and outside.

橋

Hashi
Bridge

彼岸と此岸。
「橋」という境界が、
両者の意味をゆらがせる。
今我々の属している領域は、
彼岸なのか、此岸なのか。

That shore and this shore. The boundary of a bridge unmoors the meanings of these two ideas. Where are we now—on this side or that side?

神宮内宮 宇治橋（三重県伊勢市）
Ise Shrine Inner Shrine Ujibashi (Ise, Mie Prefecture)

神宮の象徴である宇治橋は俗界と聖界を隔てる橋。渡るとここからは神苑である。冬至には橋の中央から朝日が昇ってくる。

Ujibashi Bridge, a symbol of Ise Shrine, spans the gap between the sacred and profane realms. When you cross it, you are in the sacred precincts. At the winter solstice, the sun seems to rise from the center of the bridge.

知恩院古門前の白川に架る高欄のない御影石、橋の幅は60cmほどしかない。比叡山延暦寺の千日回峰の荒修行の阿闍梨は満願のために必ず渡らなければならない橋である。

The granite bridge across Shirakawa River at Chion'in Furumonmae is only 60 centimeters wide and lacks railings.

行者橋（京都市東山区）
Gyojabashi Bridge (Arashiyama-ku, Kyoto)

橋
Hashi
Bridge

錦帯橋（山口県岩国市）
Kintaikyo Bridge (Iwakuni, Yamaguchi Prefecture)

坪庭

Tsuboniwa
Pocket Garden

ここには、世界の縮図がある。

A world in miniature.

吉田家住宅（京都市中京区）
Yoshida Residence (Nakagyo-ku, Kyoto)

黒色の加茂川石を配した鋭い造形の坪庭。

A highly sculptural pocket garden using black Kamogawa River stones.

杉本家住宅（京都市下京区）
Sugimoto Residence (Shimogyo-ku, Kyoto)

借景

Syakkei
Borrowed Landscape

庭園外の遠山や樹木を、その庭の一部であるかのように取り込む造園法。

Shakkei is A method of garden design that brings the surrounding scenery into the garden as if it were a part of the design.

日本の庭は、自己完結しない。
すべての山が、空が、宇宙が、
庭の延長にあることを知らしめてくれる。

Japanese gardens are not complete in themselves.
They tell us that all the mountains, sky, and the universe
as a whole are an extension of the garden.

尾崎家の庭は国指定の名勝で「松濤園(しょうほえん)」と呼ばれる名園である。近くまで迫った山を借景に、紀州と地元の磯の石、それに松とソテツを配した緑あふれる構成である。書院から見える山も畑もすべてが、作庭された江戸時代中期から尾崎家のものである。

The garden of the Ozaki Residence, known as Shoho-en, has been designated as a famous place of scenic beauty by the Japanese government. It borrows the landscape of the nearby mountains, and combines stones from Kishu and local ocean boulders with the rich greenery of pines and cycads. The mountain scenery and farmlands visible from the *shoin* have been in the possession of the Ozaki clan, which built the garden, since the mid-Edo period.

尾崎家住宅（鳥取県東伯郡湯梨浜町）
Ozaki Residence (Yurihama-cho, Tohaku-gun, Tottori Prefecture)

■第 5 章までの章分けは、日本の代表的な「境界」の特色をわかりやすく紹介するためにあえて分類したものである。
　例えば第 3 章「枝折戸」(p. 80) は第 1 章「門」にも分類されうるものであり、本書の分類が、各項目が保有している「境界」としての多様な意味を限定させるものではない。

Up through chapter 5, the chapters are organized to present the characteristic features of representative Japanese boundaries *(kyokai)* in an easily comprehensible manner. For example, the *shiorido* in chapter 3 (p. 80), could also be categorized in chapter 1, "Gates," and the inclusion of a feature in one chapter rather than another is not meant to be reductive.

■第 5 章までの各頁に付した用語解説は、主に以下の文献の記載を参照し作成した。
　『広辞苑 第五版』（岩波書店）
　『日本の家 空間・記憶・言葉』（TOTO 出版）
　『原色茶道大辞典』（淡交社）
　『図説・茶室の歴史 基礎がわかる Q&A』（淡交社）
　『民家（上・下）』（淡交社）
　『住まい学体系 /069 プライバシーの境界線』（住まいの図書館出版局）

Definitions of terms in the first five chapters are based on information from the following sources:
　　Kojien, fifth edition (Iwanami Shoten)
　　Nihon no Ie, Kukan, Kioku, Kotoba (TOTO Shuppan)
　　Genshoku Chado Daijiten (Tankosha)
　　Zusetsu Chashitsu no Rekishi: Kisoku ga Wakarau Q & A (Tankosha)
　　Minka (two vols) (Tankosha)
　　Sumaigaku Taikei / 069: Purabashii no Kyokaisen (Sumai no Toshokan Shuppankyoku)

■第 1 章から 5 章までのすべての写真は、高井潔氏の撮影による。また撮影地の状況解説は、撮影者本人による。

All photographs in chapters 1 through 5 are by Kiyoshi Takai, and descriptions of the site are based on information provided by the photographer.

■撮影地のうち、国指定の重要文化財・史跡名勝に選定されている場所について、一覧を設けた (pp. 140-141)。

A chart presenting the structures designated as important cultural properties and historical sites is included on pages 140–41.

第6章　現代の境界

Contemporary Boundaries

「関係性による空間構成」に挑み続ける、
3人の現代建築家による、3つのプロジェクト。
時を経た今、境界は形を変え、生き続ける。

Three projects by three contemporary architects taking on the challenge of creating space through relationships.Even today, boundaries remain an important part of the Japanese aesthetic, in new and exciting forms.

都市と森とを接続する装置
A Device Connecting the City to the Forest

隈 研吾 / 根津美術館（東京都港区）
Kengo Kuma / NEZU MUSEUN　(Tokyo, Japan)

写真：藤塚光政
Photographs by Mitsumasa Fujitsuka

単体としてのミュージアムではなく、アーバンデザインとしてミュージアムを考えたいと思った。明治神宮の杜にはじまり、ハイエンドなブランドショップがひしめき合う東京・表参道の南端を受け止めるように、根津美術館の森が緑を湛えている。根津家の私邸であった2万㎡を越す広大な敷地に、1914年の開館以来、日本・東洋古美術の優れたコレクションと、都心にいることを忘れてしまう緑豊かな日本庭園として、また庭園には茶室も点在する茶の美術館として、人々に親しまれてきた根津美術館をリニューアルして、2つの森を両端とするダンベル状の街をデザインしようと考えたのである。今回、正面道路に面して建っていた老朽化の進んだ蔵と旧館展示棟を、新しい展示棟へと建て替え、1990年増築の新館展示棟を収蔵・管理棟へと、既存建物の半分を改築し保存した。

I tried to conceive this not as an isolated museum but as a work of urban design. The forest of Nezu Museum is filled with greenery as if to absorb the impact of Omotesando, the street in Tokyo crowded with high-end brand shops that begins at the forest of Meiji Shrine and runs south in the general direction of the museum. Since opening in 1941 on a property of more than 20,000 square meters that had been the private residence of the Nezu family, the museum has become widely known for its superb collection of Japanese and Eastern antiques and a Japanese garden that is so green and tranquil that visitors may forget they are in the middle of the city; tea houses scattered throughout the garden are evidence of another area represented in the museum's collection, the arts related to the tea ceremony. On the occasion of its renewal, I conceived the idea of designing a dumbbell-shaped area, with the two forests of Meiji Shrine and Nezu Museum at its ends. The dilapidated storehouse and the old gallery building

新しい根津美術館は、都市の商業空間と森の間に、ゆるやかな勾配の屋根が生み出す影によって、周囲の環境となだらかにつながることを考えた。軒を低く抑えた折り重なる瓦屋根が、既存のイメージを継承し、新旧の建物と庭園を調和する。そうやって、リニアなエレメントの端部を森に融かしこもうとしたのである。屋根の軒先は、リン酸処理鉄板による薄さを与えることで、瓦に付随するテーマパーク的非現実感を打ち消し、研ぎ澄まされた美術品にふさわしい表情とした。外壁にも影と同質化する素材として、リン酸処理鉄板パネルを用いた。

都市に対して閉鎖的な塀で閉じるのではなく、竹林によってゆるやかに開いた、アーバンデザインとしてのミュージアムを、そのようにして街に開こうとした。人々は竹と深い庇の影の中をくぐりな

that had faced the access street were replaced by a new gallery, and the gallery addition built in 1990 was half rebuilt and half preserved to serve as a storage and administrative building.

    My intention was to gradually connect the new Nezu Museum to its environment by means of shadows produced by gently sloping roofs arranged between the commercial spaces of the city and the forest. The overlapping tiled roofs with eaves kept deliberately low maintain the museum's existing image and harmonize the buildings, new and old, with the garden. In this way, I tried to melt the ends of linear elements into the forest. By using phosphate-coated steel panels, I was able to make the roof edge thin and to negate the theme park-like air of unreality that often attaches itself to roof tiles. The result is a sharp-edged look that is appropriate to a facility dedicated to works of art. For the exterior walls I used phosphate-coated steel panels because they blend in with shadows.

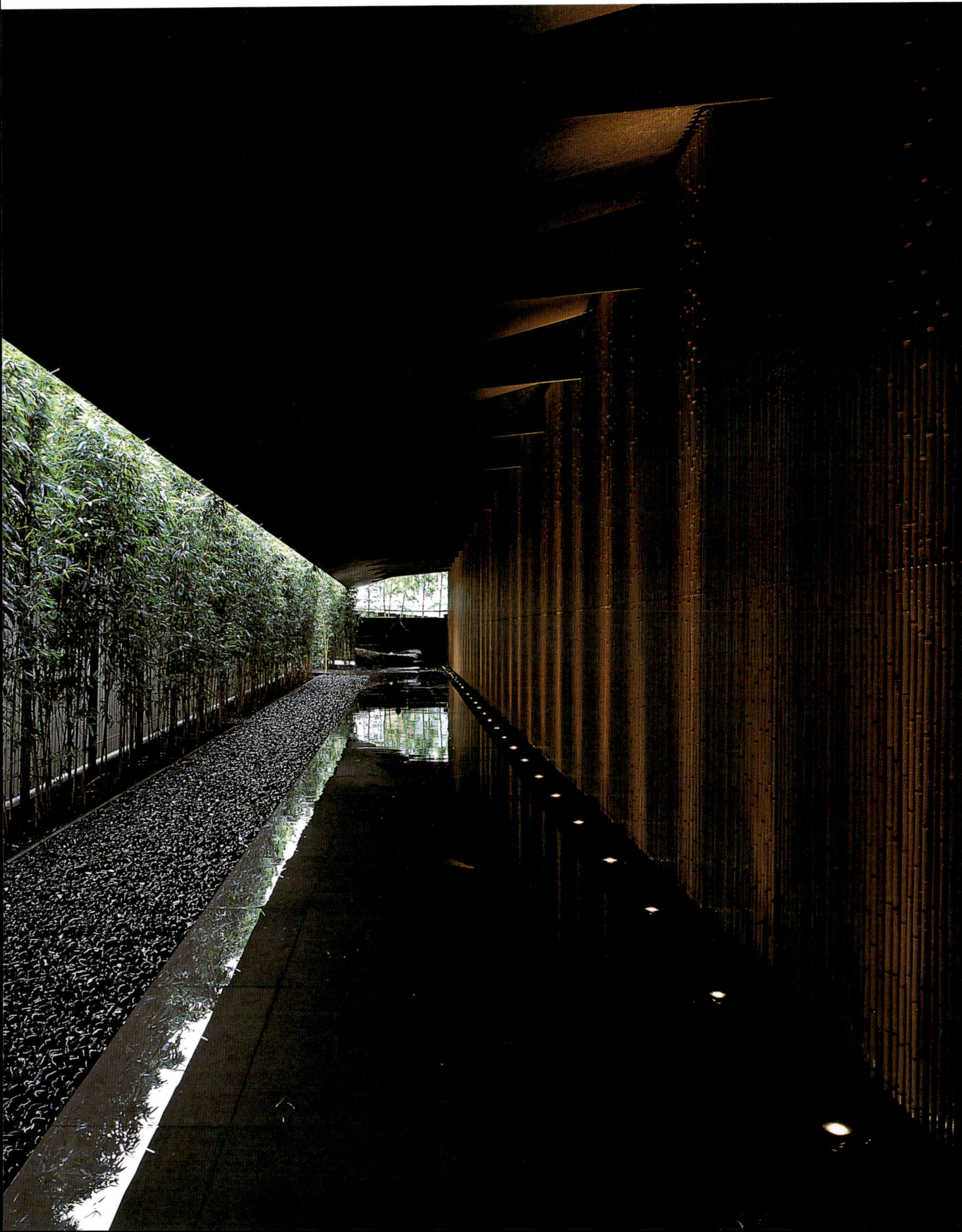

がら、都市の賑わいから美の森の中へと入っていく。茶室の露地のように、体の向きを折り返しながら、気分を切り替えていくアプローチを介して都市に接続することで、根津美術館は、明治神宮から表参道へと続いてきた都市の流れの結びとなる。

美術館内は、竹の薄板と竹林に似た表情を持つ青島(チンタオ)産の砂岩にやわらかく包まれ、大きな屋根の影の中で庭園と一体化している。内部空間も外部の大屋根に呼応する、折り重なるような斜めの天井で構成され、人々は重層する斜めの線の中を漂いながら、美に全身を浸す。

庭園の中には、根津家の温室の名残りの石垣と暖炉を保存しながら、森の自然の中で美の余韻を愉しむことのできるカフェ(写真右上)もリニューアルした。このミュージアムは都市と森とを、再び接続するための装置である。

I tried to gently open this museum-as-urban-design to the city by means of a grove of bamboo instead of closing it off from the city by a blank wall. Leaving the crowds of the city, visitors pass through the bamboos and the shadow cast by the overhanging roof and enter a forest of beauty. The approach changes direction as in a tea garden, signaling a change in mood. Through this connection to the city, Nezu Museum becomes the conclusion to the urban flow and sequence that begins at Meiji Shrine and continues on Omotesando.

The interior of the museum, gently enveloped in thin boards of bamboo and a sandstone from Qingdao whose appearance suggests a bamboo forest, is integrated with the garden in the shadow cast by the large roof. The interior spaces have overlapping diagonal ceilings that echo the large exterior roofs; wandering about under the overlapping diagonal lines, visitors immerse themselves in beauty.

In the garden, stone walls and a hearth

that remain from the Nezu family greenhouse have been preserved, and a cafe where visitors can bask in the afterglow of their encounter with beautiful works of art has been renovated. This museum is a device for reconnecting the city to the forest.

「境界」にまつわる断章
A Few Brief Words about "Boundaries"

藤本壮介 /House N（大分県）
Sou Fujimoto / House N (Oita, Japan)

写真：イワン・バーン
Photographs by Iwan Baan

ぼんやりとした境界

建築というのは、つまり内部と外部を分けるものである。内部と外部のあいだに、ある境界を設けるものだ。それは簡単なようでいて、とても難しい。今までの多くの建築がそうだったように、内部と外部のあいだを、壁によって仕切ってしまえば、それは簡単である。壁をガラスに置き換えてもいい。しかしそれでは実はもったいない。内部と外部は、0と1のようにはっきり分かれるものではない。白と黒のように明確に区別されるものでもない。むしろ、内部と外部の間には、0と1のあいだにある無数の分数、白と黒の間にある無数の色の階調が広がっているのだ。境界は1本の線ではない。ぼんやりとした境界、とでもいえるものが存在する。

Fuzzy Boundaries

Architecture is the separation of interior from exterior space. It is creating a kind of boundary between inside and outside. That seems simple, but is actually quite difficult. If walls are used to separate interior from exterior, as has been the case in most architecture up to now, establishing this boundary is simple. Glass can be used in place of opaque walls. But that is actually a terrible waste. Interior and exterior do not need to be sharply divided, like 0 and 1 in digital code, like black and white. Rather, an infinity of degrees actually exist between 0 and 1, and an infinite grading of shades exist between black and white. A boundary is not a simple line. Something we could describe as a "fuzzy boundary" can also exist.

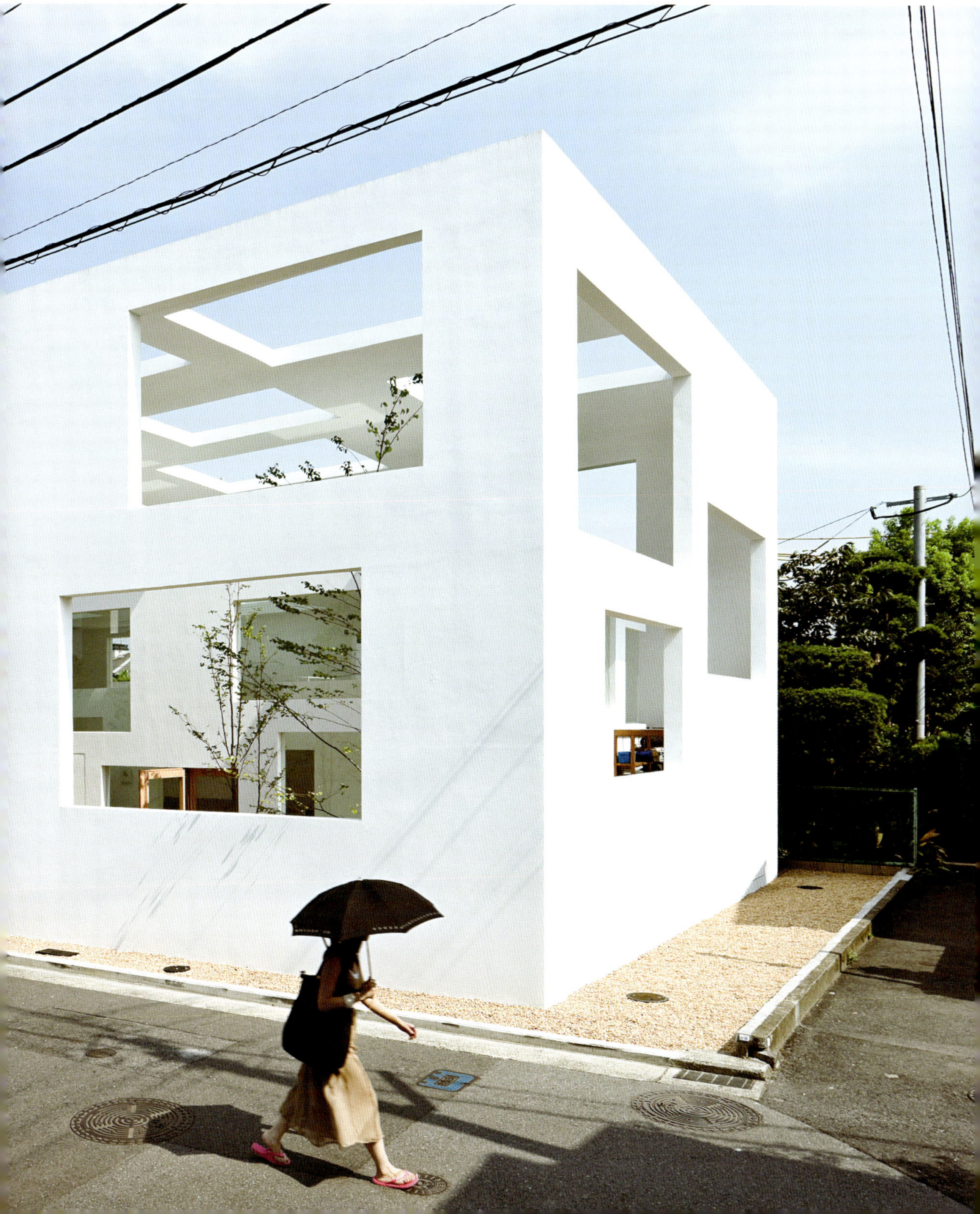

内部のような外部 / 外部のような内部

ここにあげる House N という住宅は、そのような「ぼんやりとした境界」を建築化したものである。この家は入れ子状に重なる穴だらけの3つの箱によってできている。いちばん大きな箱は敷地全体を覆っていて、その穴にはガラスがはまっていないので、この箱の内側は外部空間である。大きく囲われた庭といってもいい。2番目の箱にはガラスがはまっていて、内部空間を作り出しているが、その中にさらに小さい3つ目の箱が入っているため、家の中でありながら、家の中の中の外である、という奇妙な場所が作られている。この3つの入れ子状の箱の重なりによって、家は単に壁によって囲まれた閉じた場所ではなくなり、「だんだんと」変化していく内部から外部への領域の変化の場となる。ずいぶん奥まった内部、開いているが守られている内部、外部と内部の中間くらいの場所、おおむね外部だが、かすかに守られている場所、などなど、1本の線ではなく、ぼんやりとした境界を作ることによって、その境界の中に、今まで隠れていた様々な場所が湧きあがってくる。白と黒のあいだに隠れていた無限の色彩があふれてくる。建築がつまり境界そのものだとするなら、ぼんやりとした境界は、建築にまつわる場所の豊かさを飛躍的に拡張する可能性を持っている。

「あいだ」ということ

このぼんやりとした場の豊かさは、「あいだ」などの日本の伝統的な空間観につながっている。House N の囲まれた庭空間は、いってみれば肥大化した縁側である。外部だけれども内部的な快適さを持ち、また内部だけれども外部的な開放感がある。あいだ、というのは、たとえば内部と外部のあいだに、第3の別の場所があるというよりも、内部と外部が溶け合って、連続しながら変化している様相のことをいっているに違いない。そしてあいだ、というときに、僕たちはいわば無限の新しい場所のイメージを獲得できる。都市と住宅のあいだといってみるとき、それは未知の何かであるが、確実に空間化できそうな何かである。光と影のあいだ、透明と不透明のあいだ、内部と外部のあいだ、人工と自然のあいだ、ものと空間のあいだ、実と虚のあいだ、それらのあいだを切り開き、空間を与え、体験できるものにすることが

Interior-like Exteriors / Exterior-like Interiors

The private residence House N featured here is an example of a design with fuzzy boundaries. The basic plan is three boxes set within each other, their sides containing numerous openings of various shapes and sizes. The largest box occupies the entire site, and its apertures are open to the elements. The interior of this box is exterior space. The apertures of the second box, set within the largest, are glazed, enclosing interior space, but within this second box is yet a third, which, while set in the residence's interior, forms a strange and interesting space that is a kind of exterior within the house's interior. The placement of these three boxes one inside the other means that the residence is not simply an interior space closed off from the exterior by solid walls but is instead a gradual progression of zones from exterior to interior: an innermost interior zone, a zone that is still interior but open to the exterior, a zone that is somewhere between interior and exterior, a zone that is primarily exterior but still somewhat protected from the exterior, and so forth. Through the employment of such fuzzy boundaries rather than clear-cut lines, a range of nuanced spaces that had heretofore been hidden reveal themselves. The infinite shadings between the extremes of black and white are richly apparent. If architecture is the creation of boundaries, fuzzy boundaries have the potential for exponentially increasing the richness of architectural space.

"Between"

The richness of this fuzzy space is related to traditional Japanese concepts of space, such as intermediary zones existing between one defined space and another. The space around House N is, in a way, a giant *engawa*, the traditional Japanese veranda that separates the rooms of the house from the garden. Though it is exterior space, it possesses the comfort of interior space; while interior, it possesses the openness of the exterior. This quality of "between-ness," for example between interior and exterior, is not a third kind of space but rather a continuum between exterior and interior where the qualities of those two zones merge and gradually transition from one to the other. The word "between" suggests a limitless new zone. When we speak of "between city and house," we imagine something unknown, but something that we can conceptualize as space. Between light and shadow, between transparent and

できれば、世界はもっともっと豊かになるに違いない。

はなれていて同時につながっている

境界とは、時に何かを切り分け、時に何かをつなぎ合わせる。しかしこのぼんやりとした、グラデーションとしての境界を考えるときに、切り分けることとつなぎ合わせることは、別々のものではないのかもしれない。はなれていることとつながっていることは、別々のものではなく、むしろ表裏一体で常に入れ替わっている。完全に切り分けてしまうのでもなく、完全につながってしまうのでもない、まさにそのあいだにさまざまなつながり具合、はなれ具合の領域が広がっている。建築というのは不思議なもので、そのなんとも説明しがたい曖昧な状況を、そのまま空間として立ち上げることができる。House Nの中で過ごしているときに、街との距離感の近いような、永遠に遠いような感覚、空が時にすぐそばに見え、天井が時に無限の彼方に見える感覚。その時々によって刻々と変化する周囲の状況や人の動き、関係に応じて、はなれていることとつながっていることとは入れ替わり変化していく。

opaque, between interior and exterior, between artificial and natural, between object and empty space, between truth and falsehood—if we can cut open these intermediary zones, give them spatial form, and make them into something we can experience, our world will undoubtedly be the richer for it.

Simultaneously Separated and Connected

At different times, boundaries can both separate and connect. But when we consider the nature of fuzzy, graduated boundaries, we realize that this separation and connection are perhaps not two distinct conditions. Being separated and connected are not two different qualities but two sides of a single coin, always intermingling in reality. Instead of complete separation or connection, we discover a continuum of innumerable zones of various degrees of connection, various degrees of separation. Architecture has the mysterious ability to embody those inexplicable, ambiguous states in space. When inside House N, one feels close to the surrounding city and at the same time endlessly distant; the sky overhead is sometimes right there, and at other times the ceiling seems far, far away. The relationships arising from the changing conditions of the house's surroundings and the

森のような場所

ぼんやりとした境界、というのは、何か森のような場所であろうか。House N の中に入ったときの、周囲からどんどんはなれていく感覚と、それでいて開放的でどこまでもつながっていける感覚、自分を取り囲む場所が透明であると同時に不透明である感覚。空も含めた周囲の全体を取り込んで場が広がっていく感覚、それらは、透明な人工的な森の中にいるかのような場所の質である。森を作るとは、木を植えることではなく、また木々や森を模した建築を作ることでもない。それは透明性と不透明性が共存して常に入れ替わり、黒と白のあいだの無限の色の階調が移ろい、はなれていることとつながっていることという距離の感覚が生き生きと変化するような場所を作り出すことだ。

雲のような場所

そしてまたそれは、たとえば雲の中のような場所だといってもよい。日本の昔の屏風絵の中では、様々な情景が描かれた上に、もくもくと雲が漂っている。あの雲は雲自体を描いているというよりも、あいだで湧きおこる様々な事柄を、時につなぎ、時にはなし、関係づけていく背景のようなものであろう。虚による多様な関係性。究極の境界とは時間や空間の次元さえ異なる様々な事柄を、この雲のように様々に関係づけていく透明な存在だといえるのではないだろうか。そして未来の建築は、そんな雲のような場所になっているのかもしれない。

movement of people create a continual shift between separation and connection.

Space Like a Forest

A fuzzy boundary resembles, in a way, a forest. When you're inside House N, you experience simultaneous feelings of being separated from your surroundings, yet at the same time a freedom and endless connection, and as if the surrounding space is both transparent and opaque. A zone including the sky and everything around you seems to stretch out infinitely, creating the quality of being in some kind of transparent, man-made forest. A forest is not made by planting trees or erecting buildings imitating trees or a forest. It is made by creating a space in which transparency and opacity, the infinite graduation of shades between black and white, and the feelings of being connected and separated are constantly and dynamically shifting back and forth.

Space Like Clouds

It could also be described as like being in the clouds. On traditional Japanese folding screen paintings, the individual scenes depicted are often separated by bands of clouds. Rather than being depictions of actual clouds, they serve as a background motif that may connect, separate, or relate the scenes set between them. Their vacuity creates a diversity of relationships. The ultimate boundary, like those clouds, is a transparent thing that can establish a multiplicity of relationships, even among phenomena that exist in different temporal and spatial dimensions. The architecture of the future may well be a space like these clouds.

KAIT 工房は、大学の敷地内にキャンパス再開発の一貫として建設された、学生が好きな時に来て自主的に創作活動ができる施設である。

唐突だけれど、この建物を設計していたときに、省略するということについていろいろ考えていたことがある。たとえば、平面図上で始点と終点を決めて線を引けばひとつの面として壁が立ち上がる。その2つの点のあいだに関しては、あまりものを考えなくても一気に壁という構築物をつくりだすことができる。一般的に、ひとつの壁は同じディテールの連続でできているから、一度小さな範囲でその壁のつくり方を設計すれば大きな壁を一気に設計したことになるし、その壁が遮る向こう側の空間（もしくは、プログラム）は一時的に考えなくてもよいことになる。建築の設計は、とても大きなスケールを扱うことになるので、このように、部分、部分を多かれ少なかれ、省略しながら考え進めていくことがとくに重要なのだと思う。

そういうような構築物をつくる上での省略や、はっきりと空間を遮ることによって生まれる省略をどのように導き出すかが、建築の設計の根本的なところかもしれない。省略していくことによって、設計するなかでの思考に余白があらわれ、建物はある意味、抽象化されていく。建築の抽象性と省略はとても深い関係にあるように思う。（たとえば、ダイアグラムなどは、建築を省略し抽象的にとらえるひとつの方法である）。それは、建築を設計する上での美学にもつながっていくのだと思う。また、省略することによってつくりだされた抽象性が、建築に何か奥行きのようなものを生みだし、空間をより豊かにしていくのだと思う。しかしこの建物では、平面図上の2点間、すなわち

「省略することについて考えてみる」
Thinking about Ellipses

石上純也 / 神奈川工科大学 KAIT 工房（神奈川県厚木市）

Junya Ishigami /Kanagawa Institute of Technology KAIT workshop (Kanagawa,Japan)

写真：イワン・バーン　石上純也建築設計事務所
Photographs by Iwan Baan
junya.ishigami+associates

KAIT workshop, built as part of a campus redevelopment program at a university west of Tokyo, is a studio/workshop for the free use of students working on individual creative projects.

When I was designing the building, I was thinking about ellipses. For example, when you draw a starting point and an ending point on a plan and then connect the dots, a wall is created. Without really considering the space between the two points, the structure of a wall suddenly arises. Generally, a wall is the repetition of identical units or details, so if you design a small section of the wall, the entire thing is designed, and for the time being there's no need to consider the space—or program—on the other side of it that is delineated by the wall. Architectural design deals with space on a very large scale, so I believe it's important to think out a design by this method of eliding one part after another to a greater or lesser extent.

This basic function of architecture may indeed be the method in which this ellipses that occurs in the process of building a structure and as a result of clearly delineating space is employed. Through ellipses, blanks in the thought process taking place in the creation of the design are revealed and the work of architecture is, in a certain sense, rendered abstract. I think that abstraction and ellipses are intimately related in architecture. (For example, diagrams are a method of perceiving architecture in abstract and

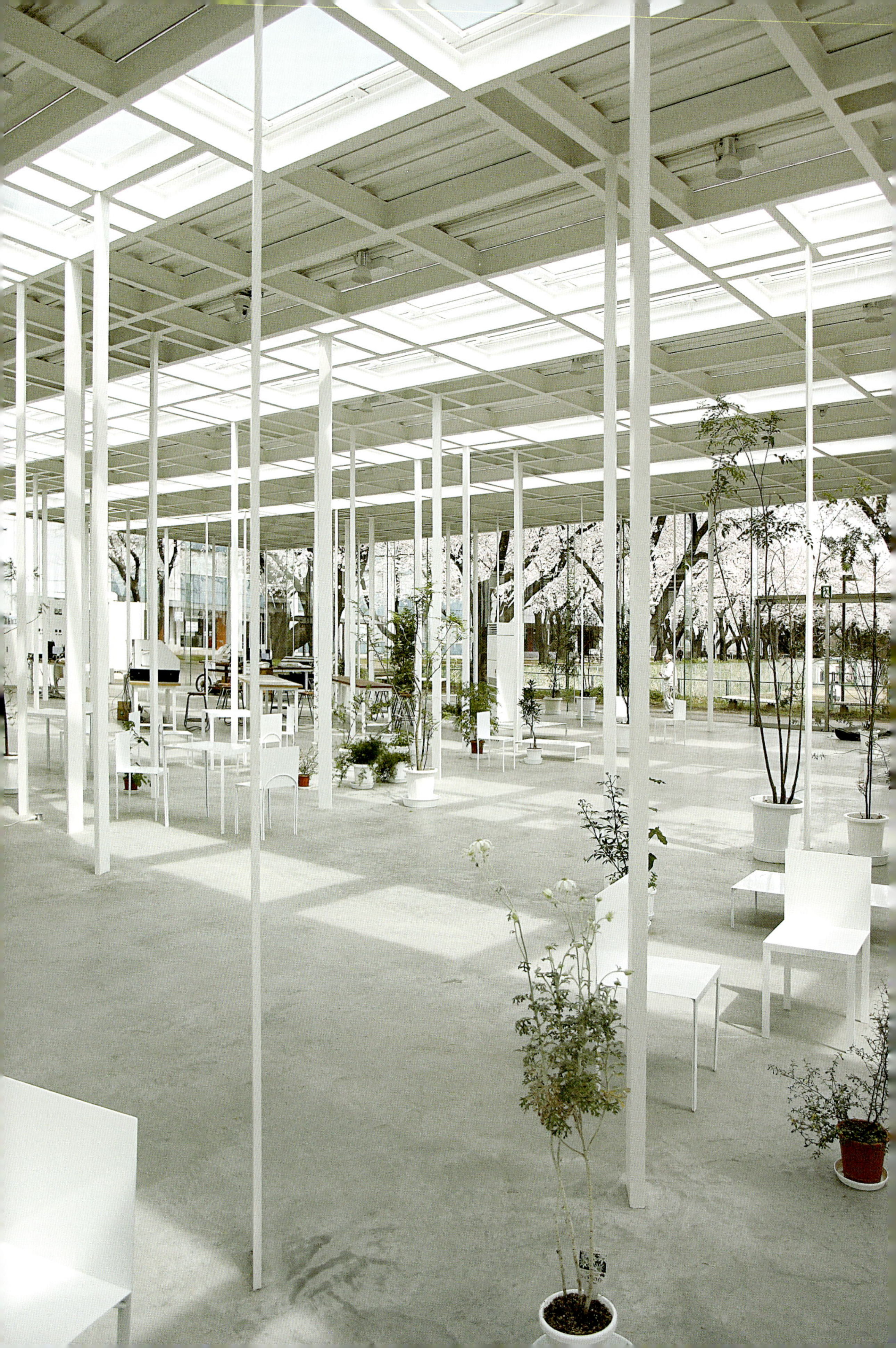

柱と柱のあいだには、ものすごく具体的な空間が広がっている。始点と終点を決めれば壁が立ち上がってきて、向こうの空間をはっきりと遮れるわけではないし、そもそも、すべての柱のプロポーションや方向は異なっている（構造の役割もそれぞれ異なっているから、構築物としての柱のタイプをひとつ決めれば、一気に他の柱の設計も出来上がるわけでもない）。この建物では、どんなに小さな範囲を設計するときでも、常に建物全体を考えながら設計を進めなければならないのである。このような省略できない、極端に具体的な空間をどのようにとらえたらよいか、どのようにしたら抽象化できるか、このプロジェクトではそういうことが大きな課題だったように思う。

そういうことをいろいろ考えているうちに、次のようなことが頭の中に思い浮かんできた。何重にも広がる具体的な空間を、ぼんやりととらえてみること。そのぼんやりしたものを何かに置き換えていくのではなく、できるだけそのままの状態で空間にしていくこと。そういうぼんやりした状態を意図的に計画することはできないだろうか。そんなことを思い始めたのである。しかしながら、少しずつ設計を進めていくうちに、そういう空間はものすごく繊細なバランスのなかで微妙にぎりぎり成り立っているものだということがだんだんとわかってきた。例えば、柱1本について考えるだけでも、その柱はそのほかの304本の柱と等価に具体的な関係を持ってしまう。その関係をある程度維持しながら、そのほかの柱も同時に調整していく。そのような膨大な情報量を一気に処理しながら空間をつくっていくような感じである。そうなってくると、演繹的に考えていたらきりがない。「イメージ」とかそういう類のものが、直接、空間や環境を形づくる目に見えないシステムに結びついていくような考え方でつくっていかなければ成り立たないのだと思うようになっていった。そしてそれが、何か新しい抽象性につながっていくような気がしていた。ダイアグラムなどが持つ抽象性とは全く異なる抽象性である。取捨選択し整理することによって得られる抽象性ではなく、どんなものでも選択可能にするような抽象性（もしくは、何も選択しなくてよい抽象性）。そういう開かれた抽象性のようなものに興味を持つようになっていった。その可能性について考えていたのだと思う。

ぼんやりとあいまいにとらえることは、いろいろな空間を単に大雑把に省略して把握する方法ではない。省

elided form.) This is also linked, I believe, to the aesthetics of architectural design. Moreover, the abstraction resulting from ellipses provides architecture with a kind of depth and resonance, enriching space.

In this building, however, the space between two points on the plan—in other words, the space between two pillars—is extremely concrete. The establishment of the two points doesn't result in a wall connecting them, and the space on either side of the line between the two points is not demarcated; the proportions and orientations of the pillars are all different (since they play differing structural roles, unlike in other structures, where the pillars play a uniform role, deciding the specifications of one pillar does not determine the specifications of all the others). In this project, the design in its entirety had to be considered when designing even the smallest unit of space. One of the major challenges of this project was how to conceptualize and abstract a work that cannot be elided and in which the space is so extremely concrete.

While considering these issues, I hit upon an idea: to conceptualize the multilayered, open, and very concrete space vaguely. And not to recast that vagueness as something else, but to preserve it in that fashion as space. Would it be possible to intentionally plan vague, unarticulated space as is? I began to think about that. But as the design advanced, I gradually came to see that the space was subtly and fully articulated in a highly sensitive balance. For example, in thinking about a single pillar, I found that it had a concrete and equal relationship with the other 304 pillars in the work. While preserving that relationship to a certain degree, the other pillars gradually came into being. It was as if I was creating the entire space at once, while processing an enormous amount of information simultaneously. Approaching this through a deductive process would have taken forever. I came to the conclusion that the only way was to come up with a thought process that brought all the information

略がないのである。省略しないで、そこにあるものをあるがままの状態で、なんとなくとらえるのである。また、具体的な省略がないからといって、それが抽象化されていないかというと、そうでもないし、なんとなくだからといっても、いい加減なわけでもない。それは、ある境界線を描くことによって空間を抽象化させる方法ではなく、とても繊細で不安定であいまいな境界をそのままの状態で抽出し、そのゆらゆらと揺らめく状態を抽象的にとらえる方法なのだと思う。この建物の場合、省略される部分は始点と終点の2点間につくられる連続した構築物（たとえば壁）のディテールでもなく、その構築物によって遮られる向こう側の空間（やプログラム）でもない。省略されるものは境界そのものである。境界がないのではなく省略されているのである。空間を遮る方法自体を無数の関係性にゆだねることで、そこに新たな質の抽象性が生まれる。

柱の配置は、一見ランダムに見えるかもしれないが、それぞれの点はかなり厳密に決められている。建築

together through some kind of intuitive system that produced space and its environment directly, something like a mental image. And it seemed to me that such a process might lead to a new kind of abstraction. It would be an abstraction completely different from that possessed by a diagram. Not an abstraction obtained by a step-by-step rational process of conscious choice and elimination, but rather an abstraction that made all choices possible (or by the same token, made it possible to make no choices). I became interested in this idea of an "open" abstraction. I was thinking about its possibility.

Perceiving in a vague and unarticulated fashion is not simply apprehending various spaces in a rough, abbreviated manner. There is no ellipses. Instead, it requires perceiving what is there in its own form, without abbreviating it, intuitively, as a whole. It is not the case that the design is not abstracted because there is not concrete ellipses, nor is it the case that an intuitive grasp of the space is in any way lacking in rigor or precision. This is not the elision of space by drawing boundaries or borders, but rather, I believe,

家の意思で、意図的に恣意的に空間がつくりだされているにもかかわらず、出来上がった建物は、それがなんの根拠で決められたのかがわからない。根拠がないように見えるが、実は、見えないだけである。その根拠が無数の関係性のなかに吸い込まれていって、認識できなくなるのである。構造なのか、機能なのか、意匠なのか、その根拠の境界さえも、繊細な揺らぎのなかに透明に溶け込んでいくとよいと考えていた。

建築をどのように省略するか。それをどのようにして建築の抽象性と結びつけるか。ぼくのなかでは、とても深く広いテーマである。

by extracting an exceedingly subtle, unstable, and vague boundary, just as it is, and capturing that gently shifting state as an abstraction. It is not that boundaries are absent, but that they are elided. The method of delineating space is left up to the infinite relationships therein, producing an abstraction of a new quality.

The positioning of the pillars may appear at first glance to be random, but in fact it has been very precisely determined. Though the space is the result of the architect's intentional and willful thought, the criteria upon which the building was designed is not apparent to the viewer. There may seem to be no criteria, but it only seems so. The criteria have been ingested by the infinite spatial relationships in the structure and are no longer perceptible. I wanted even the criteria for the boundaries between structure, function, and design to disappear into the subtle shifting of parameters.

How can architecture be elided? How can that ellipses be linked to architecture's abstraction? This is, for me, a very profound and broad theme.

指定文化財・史跡一覧
Designated Cultural Properties and Historical Sites

○指定文化財の名称については文化庁の表記にしたがった。
Names of Designated Cultural Properties are as given by the Agency for Cultural Affairs.

○物件所在地は2009年12月現在の地名表記にしたがった。
Names of locations are current as of December 2009.

○各物件に関する詳細情報については、各都道府県または市町村役場にお問い合わせください。
For detailed information, please contact the local government authorities.

※「重要文化財」とは文化財保護法の規定に基づく国指定の有形文化財を指す。

※各物件の現況は、撮影時の状況と異なっている場合がある。

pp. 20-21	旧春日大社板倉（円窓亭） Former Kasuga Shrine Wooden Storehouse	倉 Storehouse
pp. 22, 117	杉本家住宅 Sugimoto Residence	町家 Urban Dwelling
p. 22	森村家住宅 Morimura Residence	農家 Farm House
pp. 23, 53	林家住宅 Hayashi Residence	町家 Urban Dwelling
p. 24	坂野家住宅 Sakano Residence	農家 Farm House
pp. 25, 85下, 107	草野家住宅 Kusano Residence	町家 Urban Dwelling
p. 26	吉島家住宅 Yoshijima Residence	町家 Urban Dwelling
pp. 27, 62上	角屋 Sumiya	揚屋 Restaurant
p. 34	安藤家住宅 Ando Residence	農家 Farm House
p. 35	出雲大社本殿 Izumo Shrine Main Hall	神社 Shito Shrine
p. 37	上江洲家住宅 Uezu Residence	農家 Farm House
p. 39	銘苅家住宅 Mekaru Residence	農家 Farm House
p. 40	渡邊家住宅 Watanabe Residence	商家 Merchant's Residence
pp. 41-43, 97	江川家住宅 Egawa Residence	代官屋敷 Magistrate's Residence
p. 44	松延家住宅 Matsunobu Residence	商家 Merchant's Residence
p. 45	我妻家住宅 Wagatsuma Residence	農家 Farm House
p. 46	旧中村家住宅 Former Nakamura Residence	商家 Merchant's Residence
pp. 47, 67, 84, 91, 116	吉田家住宅 Yoshida Residence	商家 Merchant's Residence
pp. 48-50	渡邉家住宅 Watanabe Residence	町家 Urban Dwelling
p. 51	旧奈良家住宅 Former Nara Residence	農家 Farm House
p. 52	旧内山家住宅 Former Uchiyama Residence	農家 Farm House
p. 54	森家 Mori Residence	武家 Samurai Residence
p. 55	旧山田家住宅 Former Yamada Residence	農家 Farm House
p. 56	京都府南丹市美山町 Miyama-cho, Nantan, Kyoto	農村 Farm Village
p. 57	旧新井家住宅 Former Arai Residence	農家 Farm House
p. 58	熊谷家住宅 Kumaya Residence	商家 Merchant's Residence
p. 59	旧笹川家住宅 Former Sasagawa Residence	農家 Farm House
p. 60	旧湯川家屋敷 Former Yukawa Residence	武家 Samurai Residence
pp. 66上, 85上	喜多家住宅 Kita Residence	商家 Merchant's Residence
p. 66下	大角家住宅 Osumi Residence	商家 Merchant's Residence
p. 68	那須家住宅 Nasu Residence	農家 Farm House
p. 69	馬場家住宅 Baba Residence	農家 Farm House
pp. 70, 74	復古館頼家住宅 Fukkokan Rai Residence	町家 Urban Dwelling
p. 71	今西家書院 Imanishi Residence	町家 Urban Dwelling
p. 72	旧黒澤家住宅 Former Kurosawa Residence	農家 Farm House
p. 73	富澤家住宅 Tomizawa Residence	農家 Farm House
p. 75	堀家住宅 Hori Residence	農家 Farm House
p. 76	吉村家住宅 Yoshimura Residence	農家 Farm House
p. 78	旧矢掛本陣石井家住宅 Kuyyagake Honjin Ishii Residence	商家 Merchant's Residence
p. 79	旧目黒家住宅 Former Meguro Residence	農家 Farm House
p. 80	紫織庵（川﨑家住宅） Shiroi-an [Kawasaki Residence]	町家 Urban Dwelling
pp. 82-83	如庵 Jyo-an	茶室 Tearoom
p. 86	永富家住宅 Nagatomi Residence	農家 Farm House
p. 108	外村宇兵衛家 Tonomura Uhei Residence	町家 Urban Dwelling
p. 115	錦帯橋 Kintaikyo Bridge	橋 Bridge
pp. 118-119	尾崎家 Ozaki Residence	農家 Farm House

重要文化財	奈良市高畑町（奈良公園内）
Important Cultural Property	Takabatake-cho, Nara
市指定有形文化財	京都市下京区
Municipally Designated Tangible Cultural Property	Shimogyo-ku, Kyoto
重要文化財	奈良県橿原市
Important Cultural Property	Kashihara, Nara Prefecture
重要文化財	長野県木曾郡南木曾町
Important Cultural Property	Nagisomachi, Kiso-gun, Nagano Prefecture
重要文化財	茨城県常総市
Important Cultural Property	Joso, Ibaraki Prefecture
重要文化財	大分県日田市
Important Cultural Property	Hita, Oita Prefecture
重要文化財	岐阜県高山市
Important Cultural Property	Takayama, Gifu Prefecture
重要文化財	京都市下京区
Important Cultural Property	Shimogyo-ku, Kyoto
重要文化財	山梨県南アルプス市
Important Cultural Property	Minami Arupusu, Yamanashi Prefecture
国宝	島根県出雲市
National Treasure	Izumo, Shimane Prefecture
重要文化財	沖縄県島尻郡久米島町
Important Cultural Property	Kumejima-cho, Shimajiri-gun, Okinawa Prefecture
重要文化財	沖縄県島尻郡伊是名村
Important Cultural Property	Izena-mura, Shimajiri-gun, Okinawa Prefecture
重要文化財	千葉県夷隅郡大多喜町
Important Cultural Property	Otakimachi, Isumi-gun, Chiba Prefecture
重要文化財	静岡県伊豆の国市
Important Cultural Property	Izunokuni, Shizuoka Prefecture
重要文化財	福岡県八女郡立花町
Important Cultural Property	Tachibanamachi, Yame-gun, Fukuoka Prefecture
重要文化財	宮城県刈田郡蔵王町
Important Cultural Property	Zaomachi, Katta-gun, Miyagi Prefecture
重要文化財	岩手県盛岡市
Important Cultural Property	Morioka, Iwate Prefecture
歴史的意匠建造物	京都市中京区
Historic Building	Nakagyo-ku, Kyoto
重要文化財	新潟県岩船郡関川村
Important Cultural Property	Sekikawa-mura, Iwafune-gun, Niigata Prefecture
重要文化財	秋田県秋田市
Important Cultural Property	Akita, Akita Prefecture
登録有形文化財	富山県富山市
Registered Tangible Cultural Property	Toyama, Toyama Prefecture
名勝（知覧麓庭園）	鹿児島県南九州市
Famous Scenic Spot (Chiran Fumoto Teien)	Minami Kyushu, Kagoshima Prefecture
重要文化財	大阪府豊中市
Important Cultural Property	Toyonaka, Osaka Metropolitan District
重要伝統的建造物群保存地区	京都府南丹市
Important Traditional Building Preservation District	Nantan, Kyoto
重要文化財	埼玉県秩父郡長瀞町
Important Cultural Property	Nagatoro-cho, Chichibu-gun, Saitama Prefecture
重要文化財	山口県萩市
Important Cultural Property	Hagi, Yamaguchi Prefecture
重要文化財	新潟市南区
Important Cultural Property	Minami-ku, Niigata, Niigata Prefecture
市指定史跡	山口県萩市
Municipally Designated Historical Site	Hagi, Yamaguchi Prefecture
重要文化財	石川県石川郡野々市町
Important Cultural Property	Nonoichimachi, Ishikawa-gun, Ishikawa Prefecture
重要文化財	滋賀県栗東市
Important Cultural Property	Ritto, Shiga Prefecture
重要文化財	宮崎県東臼杵郡椎葉村
Important Cultural Property	Shiiba-mura, Usuki-gun, Miyazaki Prefecture
重要文化財	長野県松本市
Important Cultural Property	Matsumoto, Nagano Prefecture
重要文化財	広島県竹原市
Important Cultural Property	Takehara, Hiroshima Prefecture
重要文化財	奈良市福智院町
Important Cultural Property	Fukuchiin-cho, Nara
重要文化財	群馬県多野郡上野村
Important Cultural Property	Ueno-mura, Tano-gun, Gunma Prefecture
重要文化財	群馬県吾妻郡中之条町
Important Cultural Property	Nakanojomachi, Agatsuma-gun, Gunma Prefecture
重要文化財	奈良県五條市
Important Cultural Property	Gojo, Nara Prefecture
重要文化財	大阪府羽曳野市
Important Cultural Property	Habikino, Osaka Metropolitan District
重要文化財	岡山県小田郡矢掛町
Important Cultural Property	Yagakemachi, Oda-gun, Okayama Prefecture
重要文化財	新潟県魚沼市
Important Cultural Property	Uonuma, Niigata Prefecture
市指定有形文化財	京都市中京区
Municipally Designated Tangible Cultural Property	Nakagyo-ku, Kyoto
国宝	愛知県犬山市
National Treasure	Inuyama, Aichi Prefecture
重要文化財	兵庫県たつの市
Important Cultural Property	Tatsuno, Hyogo Prefecture
重要伝統的建造物群保存地区	東近江市五個荘金堂
Important Traditional Building Preservation District	Higashiomi, Shiga Prefecture
名勝	山口県岩国市
Famous Scenic Spot	Iwakuni, Yamaguchi Prefecture
名勝（松圃園）	鳥取県東伯郡湯梨浜町
Famous Scenic Spot (Shoho-en)	Yurihama-cho, Tohaku-gun, Tottori Prefecture

※日本民家集落博物館にて公開展示
On display at the Open-Air Museum of Old Japanese Farmhouses

※写真の衝立は、もともと欄間として取り付けられていた部分を修復したもの。昭和28年より設置している
The tsuitate in the photograph was reproduced from parts of a former ranma in 1953.

著者紹介
About Authors

隈 研吾 Kengo Kuma

1954 年横浜生まれ。1979 年東京大学建築学科大学院修了。コロンビア大学客員研究員を経て、2001 年より慶應義塾大学教授。2009 年より東京大学教授。1997 年「森舞台 / 登米町伝統芸能伝承館」で日本建築学会賞受賞、同年「水 / ガラス」でアメリカ建築家協会ベネディクタス賞受賞。2002 年「那珂川町馬頭広重美術館」をはじめとする木の建築でフィンランドよりスピリット・オブ・ネイチャー 国際木の建築賞受賞。近作にサントリー美術館、根津美術館。著書に『自然な建築』（岩波新書）、『負ける建築』（岩波書店）、『新・都市論 TOKYO』（集英社新書）など。

Born in Yokohama in 1954. He completed the master course in the Department of Architecture, Graduate School, Tokyo University, in 1979. After studying as a visiting scholar at Columbia University's graduate school, he became a professor at Keio University. From 2009 he has been a professor at Tokyo University. He won the Architectural Institute of Japan Award in 1997 for his Nakagawa-machi Bato Hiroshige Museum, and, the same year received the AIA Dupont Benedictus Award for his work "Water / Glass." In 2002 he was awarded the Spirit of Nature Wood Architecture Award by Finland for his wooden architecture. Among his recent works are the Suntory Art Museum and the Nezu Art Museum. His writings include *Shizen na Kenchiku* (Iwanami Shoten), *Makeru Kenchiku* (Iwanami Shoten), and *Shin Toshiron TOKYO* (Sheueisha Shinsho).

藤本壮介 Sou Fujimoto

1971 年北海道生まれ。東京大学工学部建築学科卒業後、2000 年藤本壮介建築設計事務所設立。2005 年より、若手建築家の国際的な登竜門である AR award を 3 年連続で受賞し一躍注目を浴びる。2008 年、JIA 日本建築大賞と World Architectural Festival −個人住宅部門最優秀賞。2009 年、wallpaper 誌の Design Awards 2009 を受賞。2008 年に出版された『原初的な未来の建築 Primitive Future』は、2008 年の建築書のベストセラーとなった。

Born in Hokkaido in 1971. After graduating from the Engineering Department of Tokyo University with a major in Architecture, he established the Sou Fujimoto Architectural Office in 2000. From 2005, he has been the recipient of the Architectural Review Award, an honor conferring international recognition on young architects, for three consecutive years. In 2008, he was the recipient of the Japan Institute of Architecture Award and the first prize for a design of private residence at the World Architectural Festival. In 2009 he received the Wallpaper Magazine design award. His *Genshiteki na Mirai no Kenchiku Primitive Future*, published in 2008, was a bestseller in the field of architecture.

石上純也 Junya Ishigami

1974 年神奈川県生まれ。2000 年東京藝術大学大学院美術研究科建築科修了。2000 − 04 年妹島和世建築設計事務所勤務。2004 年石上純也建築設計事務所設立。2009 年より東京理科大学非常勤講師。2008 年第 11 回ヴェネチア・ビエンナーレ国際建築展日本館にて個展。2009 年「神奈川工科大学 KAIT 工房」にて日本建築学会賞受賞。著書に『ちいさな図版のまとまりから建築について考えたこと』（INAX 出版）。

Born in 1974 in Kanagawa Prefecture. He graduated from the Arts Graduate School of Tokyo National University of Fine Arts and Music with a major in architecture in 2000. From 2000 to 2004 he worked at the Kazuyo Sejima Architectural Office, and in 2004 established his own architectural firm. From 2009 he has been a guest lecturer at Tokyo University of Science. He designed the Japanese Architect Pavilion for the 11th Venice Biennale of 2008. In 2009 he was awarded the Japan Institute of Architecture Award for his Kanagawa Institute of Technology KAIT workshop. He has authored *Chiisa na Zuhan no Matomari kara Kenchiku ni tsuite Kangaeta Koto* (INAX Shuppan).

高井 潔 Kiyoshi Takai

1938 年東京生まれ。日本大学芸術学部講師、日本写真協会理事、日本写真家協会会員。1974 年日本写真協会賞新人賞・1999 年日本写真協会賞年度賞受賞。写真集に『日本の倉』（淡交社）『民家− MINKA』（河出書房新社）『日本の民家・美と伝統』〔東日本篇・西日本篇〕（平凡社）など。著書に『建築写真術』（学芸出版社）『北京 古い建てもの見て歩き』（ダイヤモンド・ビック社）『日本の暖簾−その美とデザイン』（グラフィック社）など。写真展に「民家− MINKA」「日本の倉」「日本の建築−美と伝統の世界」など。

Born in Tokyo in 1938. A lecturer in the Nihon University Arts Department and director of the Photographic Society of Japan, he is the recipient of the society's New Artist Award and Annual Award. His photographic collections include *Nihon no Kura* (Tankosha), *Minka* (Kawade Shobo Shinsha), *Nihon no Minka: Bi to Dento, Higashi Nihon Hen, Nishi Nihon Hen* (Heibonsha), and numerous others. He has authored *Kenchiku Shashinjutsu* (Gakugei Shuppansha), *Beijing: Furui Tatemono no Mite Aruki* (Diamondo Bikku Sha), *Nihon no Sudare: Sono Bi to Dezain* (Graphic Sha), and others. Among his many photographic exhibitions are "Minka," "Nihon no Kura," and "Nihon no Kenchiku: Bi to Dento no Sekai."

写真
Photo Credits

p. 16	宮内庁京都事務所	Kyoto Office, Imperial Household Agency
pp. 20-119	高井潔	Kiyoshi Takai
pp. 122-127	藤塚光政	Mitsumasa Fujitsuka
pp. 128-135, 137, 138	イワン・バーン	Iwan Baan
pp. 136, 139	石上純也建築設計事務所	junya.ishigami+associates

翻訳
Translation

ジェフェリー・ハンター	Jeffrey Hunter
渡辺 洋	Hiroshi Watanabe (pp. 6-18, 122-127)

装幀
Book Design

鈴木正道 (Suzuki Design)	Masamichi Suzuki

謝辞
Acknowledgements

本書の制作にあたり、多大なご協力を賜りました下記の諸機関、関係者各位に厚く御礼申し上げます。
We would like you to express our sincere gratitude to all the following for their generous assistance and contributions to the production of this book.

隈研吾建築都市設計事務所
Kengo Kuma & Associates

藤本壮介建築設計事務所
Sou Fujimoto Architects

石上純也建築設計事務所
junya.ishigami+associates

青木一平
出雲大社社務所
江川邸公開事務室
鹿島出版会
株式会社萬養軒
株式会社名鉄犬山ホテル
宮内庁京都事務所
熊谷美術館
財団法人今西家保存会
財団法人角屋保存会
財団法人奈良屋記念杉本家保存会
神宮司庁
神護寺
高山稲荷神社
知覧武家屋敷庭園保存会
日本民家集落博物館

根津美術館
ハイアットリージェンシー京都
八幡宮
法然院
松本市立博物館
丸榮株式会社
三木竹材店
水海道風土博物館坂野家住宅
無名舎 吉田家住宅
矢掛本陣を守る会
旅館鶴富屋敷
早稲田大学理工学術院創造理工学部建築学科 中谷研究室
渡邉家保存会

文化財保有者各位
教育委員会ならびに文化財担当者各位

境界
世界を変える日本の空間操作術

2010年 3月14日 初版発行
2025年 5月 5日 六版発行

著者　　　隈研吾　高井潔
発行者　　伊住公一朗
発行所　　株式会社 淡交社
本社　　　〒603-8588　京都市北区堀川通鞍馬口上ル
　　　　　営業 075-432-5156
　　　　　編集 075-432-5161
支社　　　〒162-0061　東京都新宿区市谷柳町 39-1
　　　　　営業 03-5269-7941
　　　　　編集 03-5269-1691
　　　　　www.tankosha.co.jp
印刷・製本　TOPPANクロレ株式会社

Ⓒ2010 淡交社 Printed in Japan
ISBN978-4-473-03645-2

定価はカバーに表示してあります。
落丁・乱丁本がございましたら、小社書籍営業部宛にお送りください。
送料小社負担にてお取り替えいたします。
本書のスキャン、デジタル化等の無断複写は、著作権法上での例外を除き禁じられています。
また、本書を代行業者等の第三者に依頼してスキャンやデジタル化することは、いかなる場合も著作権法違反となります。